the **Ab🔘ut**.com guide to

FAMILY CRAFTS

**Over 150 Simple and Fun Projects
Everyone Can Make Together**

Sherri Osborn

Adams Media
Avon, Massachusetts

About About.com

About.com is a powerful network of more than 600 Guides—smart, passionate, accomplished people who are experts in their fields. About.com Guides live and work in more than twenty countries and celebrate their interests in thousands of topics. They have written books, appeared on national television programs, and won many awards in their fields. Guides are selected for their ability to provide the most interesting information for users, and for their passion for their subject and the Web. The selection process is rigorous—only 2 percent of those who apply actually become Guides. The following are some of the most important criteria by which they are chosen:

- High level of knowledge/passion for their topic
- Appropriate credentials
- Keen understanding of the Web experience
- Commitment to creating informative, actionable features

Each month more than 48 million people visit About.com. Whether you need home-repair and decorating ideas, recipes, movie trailers, or car-buying tips, About.com Guides can offer practical advice and solutions for everyday life. Wherever you land on About.com, you'll always find content that is relevant to your interests. If you're looking for "how to" advice on refinishing your deck, About.com will also show you the tools you need to get the job done. No matter where you are on About.com, or how you got here, you'll always find exactly what you're looking for!

About Your Guide

 Sherri Osborn is an avid crafter who lives in beautiful northern Minnesota with her kids, husband, and several pets. Her love of crafting began when she was a child, and through the years she has enjoyed experimenting with many craft techniques and media. She enjoys sharing her love of crafting with everyone.

She ran her own home day care business for several years and also worked at an elementary school, but now she concentrates all of her energy on the success of the About.com Family Crafts Web site (http//:familycrafts.about.com) and a few other creative ventures.

She started writing for About.com in 1997 (then called The Mining Company), where she was in charge of the Day Care/Child Care site. In 1999 she took over the Crafts for Kids site, which became Family Crafts in 2001.

She has taken various classes to learn different craft techniques, and her crafts have been featured in various craft shows and magazines. She has also worked as both a contributing author and developmental editor on several craft books.

Acknowledgments

I would like to thank my husband, Charlie, and kids, Katie, Chris, and Joey, who are always my inspiration and were neglected on occasion when I locked myself in my office to work on this book. My kids are also my guinea pigs when it comes to testing some of my craft projects. Thanks, also, to my mother, Carren, and grandmothers, Betty and Ardie, for all of the creative opportunities they have provided.

ABOUT.COM

CEO & President
Scott Meyer

COO
Andrew Pancer

SVP Content
Michael Daecher

Director, About Operations
Chris Murphy

Marketing Communications
Manager
Lisa Langsdorf

ADAMS MEDIA

Editorial

Publishing Director
Gary M. Krebs

Managing Editor
Laura M. Daly

Acquisitions Editor
Brielle K. Matson

Development Editor
Katie McDonough

Marketing

Director of Marketing
Karen Cooper

Assistant Art Director
Frank Rivera

Production

Director of Manufacturing
Susan Beale

Production Project Manager
Michelle Roy Kelly

Senior Book Designer
Colleen Cunningham

About.com® is a registered trademark of About, Inc.

Published by Adams Media, an F+W Publications Company
57 Littlefield Street
Avon, MA 02322
www.adamsmedia.com

ISBN-10: 1-59869-346-8
ISBN-13: 978-1-59869-346-1

Printed in China.

J I H G F E D C B A

Library of Congress Cataloging-in-Publication Data
is available from the publisher.

This publication is designed to provide accurate and authoritative information with regard to the subject matter covered. It is sold with the understanding that the publisher is not engaged in rendering legal, accounting, or other professional advice. If legal advice or other expert assistance is required, the services of a competent professional person should be sought.
—From a *Declaration of Principles* jointly adopted by a Committee of the American Bar Association anda Committee of Publishers and Associations

Many of the designations used by manufacturers and sellers to distinguish their product are claimed as trademarks. Where those designations appear in this book and Adams Media was aware of a trademark claim, the designations have been printed with initial capital letters.

Illustrations by Eric Andrews

This book is available at quantity discounts for bulk purchases. For information, please call 1-800-289-0963.

How to Use This Book

Each About.com book is written by an About.com Guide—an expert with experiential knowledge of his or her subject. While the book can stand on its own as a helpful resource, it can also be coupled with the corresponding About.com site for even more tips, tools, and advice. Each book will not only refer you back to About.com, but it will also direct you to other useful Internet locations and print resources.

All About.com books include a special section at the end of each chapter called Get Linked. Here you'll find a few links back to the About.com site for even more great information on the topics discussed in that chapter. Depending on the topic, you could find links to such resources as photos, sheet music, quizzes, recipes, or product reviews.

About.com books also include four types of sidebars:

- **Ask Your Guide:** Detailed information in a question-and-answer format
- **Tools You Need:** Advice about researching, purchasing, and using a variety of tools for your projects
- **Elsewhere on the Web:** References to other useful Internet locations
- **What's Hot:** All you need to know about the hottest trends and tips out there

Each About.com book will take you on a personal tour of a certain topic, give you reliable advice, and leave you with the knowledge you need to achieve your goals.

CONTENTS

CONTENTS . . . *continued*

Introduction from Your Guide

I think it is safe to assume that everyone knows what crafts are, but I would be willing to bet that different people would explain crafts in different ways. Crafts have different meanings to different people, stemming from their early experiences with crafts and their current preferences.

One of my goals with both this book and my Web site is to give parents, grandparents, and others who spend a lot of time with children some tools and motivation to help them create warm memories and positive crafting experiences with their children. By spending quality time together doing crafts now, you will be fostering a lifelong love for creative challenges in your child.

This book is not meant to simply give you page after page of step-by-step projects. It is meant more as a guide to encourage you to try different crafts with your children and allow them to experiment with different techniques. My hope is that you will try the different crafts presented here and then do some additional exploring to find more projects involving the techniques and craft products you enjoyed working with most. You can find a large selection of free projects on my About.com Web site at http://family crafts.about.com. You can also see colored photos of all of the projects in this book. As an added bonus, you can submit pictures of the crafts you complete using the directions found at http://about. com/familycrafts/shareideas.

There are many things children can learn by doing crafts. Most importantly, crafting teaches kids to take pride in their work, stretches their imaginations, and gives them the feeling of success that comes with creating. While I believe the emphasis while doing arts and crafts projects should be put on the process itself, I think it is also a good lesson for kids on following through and finishing projects.

There is no specific age your child should be before she starts crafting. When my daughter was one and a half years old, she would sit for long periods of time in her high chair, using color crayons to scribble on paper. The youngest kids are also fascinated by clay, painting, stringing large beads, and anything you can create that will make noise! The best judge as to whether your child can handle doing crafts or not is you. Your goal is to have your little one enjoy himself without getting frustrated. You will be amazed at how much he can do once you start introducing him to various craft items.

Be sure to encourage your child's creativity, and try not to have expectations of how the finished artwork should look. Often a child sees the world from a different point of view. Remember, there really is no right way or wrong way to make crafts. If you are working on a craft with a young child, try not to do identical craft projects. Children need time to develop their creative skills without being discouraged by comparisons to adult projects.

Doing crafts together makes for great quality time for children and parents. Plus, it gives parents a chance to see the world through their kids' eyes, and hopefully to remember what it is like to act like a child—sometimes one of the biggest challenges a parent faces.

I believe that when given the proper encouragement, materials, and patience, a person of any age can accomplish amazing things. As a parent, I urge you to keep this in mind when doing craft sessions with your children. Allow your children to show you how amazing they can be, and hopefully they will look back on their crafting experiences with fond memories.

Chapter 1

Getting Started with Family Crafts

A Crafter's Toolbox

Whether you are already an avid crafter or are just starting out, a well-stocked craft toolbox is a must. As you go along, you may realize you need several toolboxes—and bins, baskets, and boxes—to hold all of your supplies, but for now you can start with the basics.

Actual toolboxes are great for craft supplies because they usually have many levels and compartments. You may find these compartments really handy for holding smaller items, like buttons or beads. However, if you're not in the mood to invest in a traditional toolbox, you can use whatever you have around the house. Cardboard boxes, jars with lids, and plastic containers all work well. If you are really lucky, you can devote an entire cupboard, closet, or even an entire room to your craft tools and supplies.

▶ While I do use toolboxes for some smaller craft supplies, the main items I use for storing are large plastic bins. The ones I use the most are 18-gallon, covered plastic tubs like those made by Rubbermaid (www.rubbermaid .com). You can get them in a variety of colors, but I prefer the clear ones so I can see exactly what is inside. I put a piece of masking tape on the side so I can keep a list of everything inside it.

While some of the items you will put in your craft toolbox may vary depending on the crafts you enjoy doing, there are some basic supplies you should try to keep on hand. Most people will use all of these items in their craft projects at some time or another, and you will probably find that you use some basic supplies more than others. One thing is for sure: If you have a good collection of the basics on hand, you will be ready to go whenever the urge to create hits you.

The first thing you should add to your toolbox is a notepad and pen or pencil. This will help you stay organized. You can keep lists of craft supplies you want to add to your collection, products you really like and want to buy again, or brands you don't care for. It is also nice for keeping notes about crafts you have already made and also about craft projects you want to try. I also keep a small notebook in my purse in case I get inspiration when I'm out and about.

Paper is definitely a necessity, but what kind? There are plenty to choose from; you can find everything from plain, white copy paper to fancy sheets of archival-quality scrapbook paper. The following few types, however, will be a good start:

- **Bond paper:** Plain, white paper you can use for drawing or just about anything else
- **Construction paper:** Economical paper, usually colored, sold in larger packs or in notebook form
- **Cardstock:** Heavy-weight paper, commonly used in making cards, business cards, postcards, and more

Stock a variety of writing and coloring instruments. There are many different types of writing and drawing utensils out there, but as a beginning crafter you really only need a few to get started: pencils, crayons, and markers. While you may be tempted to buy every color of the rainbow right away, I would encourage you to let your arsenal of writing and coloring instruments grow over time. Start with the basics and then add more colors and styles as you go.

Paint is another essential craft supply. The paint you will use, and the tool you will use to apply it, will depend on the project itself. These are the ones I always have in my craft toolbox:

- **Acrylic paint:** This is usually my first choice for any project. It is a quick drying, water-soluble paint, but durable and hard to remove once dried.
- **Tempera paint:** A quick-drying, water-based paint that is great for kids, because it is easy to wash off of anything it may get on. In fact, you can add a few drops of dish soap to the paint itself to make it even easier to clean up.
- **Finger paint:** This is a popular choice with kids, and those of us who are kids at heart. This paint has the consistency of jelly, and is usually shiny once dry.
- **Dimensional paint:** A versatile paint that is high quality and slow drying that usually comes in a squeeze bottle. It is great for creating a raised 3D design on any project, and can be used on just about any surface.

Adhesives are what we use to stick one item to another. Years ago, the basics would have been a bottle of white glue and a roll of cellophane tape. Today, there are special glues and tapes to stick just about anything to just about anything else. Here is a list of basic glue products to get you started:

ELSEWHERE ON THE WEB

▶ Think all paper is the same? Think again! You can find dozens of different kinds of paper used for dozens of different purposes. Just look at all that is offered at www .paper.com. With the popularity of scrapbooking and card making, some stores have started carrying rows and rows of fancy, printed paper. You can find paper in a variety of thicknesses, colors, and even printed with designs for just about any theme you can think of.

▶ Some of the most popular pages on my Web site are the free, printable coloring-book pages. I have over 100 original, printable coloring-book pages posted, plus links to several hundred more. You can browse through an alphabetical listing of all of the coloring pages, or you can browse through a listing by topic. There is also an article explaining the best way to print them: http://about.com/familycrafts/coloringpages.

- **Craft glue:** If you will only have one type of glue in your toolbox, this should be it. It is a thick, white glue that holds better than white school glue. It is great for gluing heavier items. I use it for almost everything! This glue is also referred to as Tacky Glue.
- **White school glue:** A quick drying, versatile adhesive that can also be used as a sealant.
- **Glue stick:** A semi-solid glue that comes in a tube that can be held and used like a writing instrument. Good for kids and working with paper, cardboard, and photos.
- **Hot glue:** Sold in round "sticks" and applied with a hot glue gun. This should be used only with close adult supervision, because it gets very hot. This is good for tacking items together, but not necessarily for a permanent hold. It may not bond to all surfaces, and it does not give a smooth application. I usually add a little bit of craft glue when I use hot glue sticks to give it more of a permanent hold.

As far as tape goes, you really only need two types when you get started with crafts: cellophane tape, a stronger, transparent tape; and double-sided adhesive, which usually comes in a roll, like tape, but with the adhesive on both sides.

There are all sorts of cutting tools. The most popular has got to be a plain, old-fashioned pair of scissors, but today you have several choices, even when it comes to scissors. Start out with a cheap pair of scissors you can use to cut just about anything and expand from there. Children should always be closely supervised while using any sort of cutting tool, and should not use any of the cutting tools that are razor sharp.

Here are three basic cutting tools to get you started:

- **Scissors:** Choose the type that suits your needs, including child-safe varieties. I have one pair I use for paper, another pair I use for fabric, and a third pair for everything else.
- **Paper hole puncher:** These hand-held hole punchers used to come mainly in plain circle designs, but with the variety of hole punchers on the market today, you can make holes in your paper projects in just about any shape and size.
- **Utility knife:** This is usually a pointy razor blade with a handle that you can use to cut detailed pieces of paper and shapes using stencils, and also cut cardboard and other thicker items. These should be used with a cutting mat and should never be left out or used where little fingers can get near them.

Every crafter should keep a variety of embellishing supplies handy. Pick out your favorites and then add more as you expand your toolbox. All of these are versatile and can be used for a variety of projects:

- **Beads:** Choose whatever catches your eye! The two most popular types are pony beads and seed beads.
- **Chenille stems:** These are also referred to as pipe cleaners. They come in a large variety not only of colors, but also styles, such as metallic, bumpy, and loopy.
- **Craft foam:** They now make craft foam in a large selection of precut sheets, but if you have several different colored sheets around you can make your own shapes.
- **Craft sticks:** You can do many things with these popsicle-style sticks.

ASK YOUR GUIDE

What can I do about the stringy trails left behind by the hot glue gun?

▶ You can try two different things. First, keep your glue sticks in the freezer until you are ready to use them; doing this is supposed to reduce the strings. After you use the glue sticks, you can wave a hair dryer on a low setting over the strings to make them curl up and disappear.

▶ I highly recommend that everyone use an apron or a smock while crafting—no matter what your age. I cannot tell you how often I have seen clothing ruined by spilled supplies. You do not have to go out and buy a fancy apron or artist smock; you can use an old garment hanging in your closet. Worn button-down shirts work well (kids can wear them backwards), and oversized T-shirts are another great option.

- **Felt:** This is available in 8.5" × 11" sheets or by the yard. It is also available in a few different varieties, like glitter or fur.
- **Glitter:** Sometimes messy, but always fun.
- **Magnets:** You can get these in strips, sheets, or buttons, and some of them already have adhesive applied to one side.
- **Pom-poms:** Like many of the other items listed here, these are available in a large variety of colors, sizes, and styles, and can be bought in a mixed package.
- **Wiggle eyes:** You can also buy a variety pack of these to ensure a nice selection to choose from.
- **Yarn:** You never know when you will need a little hunk of yarn.

A few more basics can round out any crafter's toolbox. You may already have some of these things lying around your house:

- **Freezer paper:** Great for tracing patterns, because it can be temporarily stuck to almost any fabric with a hot iron.
- **Wax paper:** A great work surface—even dried glue can be gently pried off of it.
- **Clear acrylic spray:** Great for adding a protective top coat to painted and other finished projects; it can be used for a glossy or matte protective surface.
- **Cutting mat:** For use with rotary cutters or utility knives.
- **Ruler:** You will find you have many occasions for measuring while you're making crafts.
- **Tweezers:** A great tool when you are working with small items.

Beyond the Basics

Once you have your toolbox stocked with basic supplies, you can move on to supplies that are a little more advanced or specialized.

Some of these you may not use, but most you will have some use for while doing many crafts. What you choose beyond the basics might depend on what kind of crafts you prefer to do.

Are you ready to take your paper to the next level? Though the classics like plain white paper and construction paper may be foremost in your mind, there are quite a few different papers available to you for crafts. The following are a few types you may want to add to your toolbox:

- **Finger-paint paper:** Paper with a coated, nonabsorbent surface that allows for fast drying and holds up well to the thickness of finger paint
- **Vellum:** A heavy-weight paper that comes in various degrees of transparency, great for making cards and other paper crafts
- **Tracing paper:** A thin, translucent paper usually used over a light source for tracing patterns
- **Blank newsprint:** A low-cost, unbleached paper that comes in a variety of sizes; it is popular in larger sizes for use on a child's easel
- **Tag board:** A lightweight cardboard suitable for making signs and posters that comes in a variety of sizes, colors, and styles
- **Archival paper:** Paper that is acid free, lignin free, and resists fading, commonly used in scrapbooking and other projects meant to last many years

Experiment with a variety of writing and coloring instruments. There are plenty of options beyond plain pencils and crayons. Consider adding these options to your toolbox:

ELSEWHERE ON THE WEB

▶ One of my favorite craft Web sites is called Create For Less (www.createforless .com). This is an online craft store where you can shop by department, brand, craft type, occasion, or theme. The prices are usually comparable to or cheaper than those you would encounter elsewhere. They also have a large selection of Girl Scout themed items. Their advice column is also a wonderful tool.

▶ Chalk is not just for chalk-boards and sidewalks! Think beyond the little sticks of chalk many of us are familiar with and explore the cases full of colorful chalk available at craft stores. Chalk is popular in paper projects, where it is used to add high-lights and shading. Another popular use is with stuffed animals and dolls, as it is a great way to add a little color to chubby cheeks.

- **Colored pencils:** These are great for coloring and shading and also for kids who think they are too old for crayons
- **Chalk:** Chalk can be used for writing and drawing and also for shading and adding dabs of color in a variety of projects
- **Ink pads:** Not only can you use them with rubber stamps, you can use them to make prints with other objects
- **Charcoal:** A drawing pencil or crayon made from a black, porous material that smudges easily
- **Pastels:** These look similar to crayons but are closer in consistency to chalk, and can also easily be smudged

The paint you will want to use may vary depending on your project. While I almost always turn to my acrylic or dimensional paint when working on projects, there are other paint products that can be handy:

- **Watercolors:** Cakes of dried paint usually applied with a wet brush that dry quickly to a thin, dull finish
- **Food coloring:** Can be mixed with water and used like watercolors, except these stain
- **Spray paint:** The paint is sprayed onto the surface, usually from a can, and is great for covering large areas or getting to those hard-to-reach places
- **Glass paint:** Smooth, transparent paint that allows light to shine through

Sometimes you need to reach beyond the basics when it comes to adhesives. Choosing the right glue can save you a lot of headaches in the long run. When one of your basic glues or tapes won't do, try one of these:

- **Strong glue:** Industrial-strength, slow-drying glue used to glue together hard-to-stick or heavy items and items that need a little more support. It is best to use clamps until items dry. I prefer to use either E6000 or Gorilla Glue brands.
- **Super glue:** Thin, very quick-setting glue. This glue is not as strong as slower-drying glues.
- **Duct tape:** Also called duck tape, this gray tape is strong, fabric-based, and multi-purpose.
- **Glitter glue:** Flecks of colored glitter that is suspended in liquid glue or embedded in a hot glue stick. You can glue and embellish at the same time.
- **Masking tape:** Usually beige or blue in color, this tape is made of easy-to-tear paper that is backed with a relatively weak adhesive.
- **Spray adhesive:** This adhesive is applied from an aerosol can, and can be permanent or temporary.

You can add some fun details to projects using different cutting tools. While most cutting can be accomplished with a pair of scissors, some of these cutting tools will help make your cutting jobs a little easier:

- **Paper trimmers:** These are great for trimming papers or photos and creating nice, straight edges. This tool has a razor-sharp blade that slides over the paper.
- **Pinking shears:** These scissors have a zigzag cutting edge and are used mostly with fabric crafts.
- **Rotary cutter:** A tool that looks like a pizza cutter, with a rolling, razor-sharp blade. It is usually used with a straight-edge ruler and cutting mat to cut fabrics.

TOOLS YOU NEED

▶ You may think you need fancy applicators and brushes to work with paint, chalk, and even glue, but think again! One of the best tools I have used to apply all three of these products is a simple cotton swab. You can also use fingertips, sponges, foam brushes, straws, and tooth-brushes. Dig around your junk drawers at home and see what else you can find!

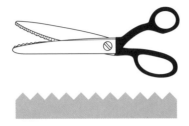

◀ Pinking shears make a
zig-zag cut

▶ Have you walked down
the button aisle of your
favorite craft store lately?
Based on the huge selection
offered, it is safe to assume
that this is one of the most
popular crafting products
available. Buttons are not just
round anymore; they come
in many shapes and colors,
and are also available in a
large assortment of themed
designs. Use them to adorn
paper or fabric projects, as
well as other projects, like
those featured at http://about
.com/familycrafts/usebuttons.

You can personalize all of your projects using unique embellishments. Some of these may not seem like traditional craft supplies, but you will be happy to have them on hand when you need them:

- **Bells:** Both small and large jingle bells make nice embellishments.
- **Brads:** Paper brads are not only nice for holding pieces of paper together, they can also add a nice decorative element.
- **Buttons:** Whether sewn or glued onto projects, these make great accents.
- **Clothespins:** There are a variety of crafts you can make using either the old-fashioned style or ones with springs.
- **Contact paper:** Among its many other uses, clear contact paper can be used as a protective laminate for projects. Colored contact paper can be used to create personalized stencils that can be stuck to projects and then easily removed.
- **Craft wire:** This fancy wire is available in a wide array of colors and gauges.
- **Elastic:** I like to keep a variety of thicknesses on hand, but especially useful is elastic thread that can be used to make simple jewelry and other craft items.
- **Feathers:** A nice embellishment option.

- **Plaster of Paris:** Used for making special keepsakes, in molds, and much more.
- **Rhinestones/gems:** Usually flat on one side, these can be used to embellish just about anything.
- **Ribbon and lace:** These can be used to dress up many projects. Plastic lace is great for lanyards, lacing projects, and jewelry.
- **Sequins:** Use sequins to add sparkle and interest to your crafts.
- **Stickers:** These are great to have on hand for quick embellishing, and they provide a great option for younger kids who have a hard time using glue or double-sided tape.
- **String/twine:** You just never know when you might need a piece!
- **Styrofoam shapes:** You can find Styrofoam in a variety of shapes and sizes.

Do you have any room left in your toolbox? If so, some of the following items might be good to have on hand:

- **Needle-nose pliers:** These make grabbing and holding small items easier.
- **Pushpins:** These are handy for holding items in place or hanging up your work in progress to get a better look at it.
- **Rubber stamps:** You can get a variety of designs to use in most crafts.
- **Safety pins:** Great for holding items together.
- **Stapler:** For use when glue and tape just won't do the job.
- **Suction cups:** A fun way to hang up finished projects!
- **Tape measure:** For when you need to measure bigger objects.
- **Wire cutters:** Used for cutting wire so you don't ruin your scissors.

Where do you get your inspiration and ideas for craft projects?

▶ I have a huge collection of craft books and magazines. I also enjoy going to craft stores and walking up and down all of the aisles to see what catches my eye. Some of the craft projects I come up with are inspired by need, like a bare wall that needs something hanging on it. I also get ideas from questions asked by visitors to my Web site.

Specialty Supplies and Fun Gadgets

There are new specialty tools, crafting gadgets, and gimmicks coming out all of the time. Avoid buying items that seem too good to be true, and be leery of products made by manufacturers you have never heard of. For items that have a higher price tag, make sure you do your research.

I would like to share a few specialty gadgets that I think are worthy of your consideration and the money they cost. I also wanted to mention a few of my favorite supplies and tools that don't cost a lot of money. Most of these have been around for quite awhile, and while their popularity may come and go, they have withstood the test of time.

Shrink plastic, a sheet of thin, flexible plastic that you draw or color on, cut shapes out of, and then place it in a pre-heated oven, can be enjoyed by all ages. I remember using shrink plastic to make crafts when I was a child, and its popularity has come and gone a few times since then. As an adult, I have a whole new respect for the concept and the possibilities this product presents. While shrink plastic used to be readily available in only translucent sheets, it can now be purchased in a handful of colors. You can now also buy shrink plastic that you can use with your computer printer.

Polymer clay can be used as an embellishment or to make a project. This is a little more sophisticated than the clay many children play with. Polymer clay does not dry out like play clay; it remains pliable until it is baked in an oven. It is fairly easy to work with and very fun to experiment with. It can be sculpted, carved, stamped, sanded, and painted. You can make anything you can think of—from miniatures to jewelry.

A light box can be used for a variety of purposes. It is a back-lit frame with a translucent face of plastic or glass used to transmit light through an image for the purpose of tracing and slide viewing. It can also be used with embossing to view the stencil lines under the sheet of paper. My kids have discovered my light box and now use it all of the time to trace cartoons and other items.

Once you own a laminator you will wonder what you ever did without it. I have a small, no-heat laminator, and I love playing with it. I have used it to seal photos for my husband to carry in his wallet and to make fun tags. It can be used to seal and protect a wide variety of items, as long as they are fairly flat. This is definitely a luxury tool, but we all deserve a little luxury in our lives!

A sticker maker can add a new depth to your crafting. You also have a few choices when it comes to brands of sticker makers—just remember that you get what you pay for. This little machine lets you use your own photographs, clip art, or even pictures cut from magazines and catalogs to make personalized stickers. Adults will have as much fun with this as the kids.

You can use a die cut machine to make fancy shapes using paper or fabric. This wonderful tool will cost you a little more than the others we have talked about so far, but is worth the cost. Die cut machines are used to cut specific shapes out of paper and fabric by using a die to cut the paper into the desired shape by using pressure. A very simplistic way to explain it may be to compare it to a cookie cutter. When it comes to choosing a die cut machine, there are many brands, sizes, and styles to choose from. They range from smaller, handheld models that are fairly

TOOLS YOU NEED

▶ If you would like several fun craft gadgets in one machine, you might want to invest in a Xyron. The Xyron can turn pictures into stickers, make magnets and labels, and do cold laminating. It is refillable and uses no heat, electricity, or batteries. Not only are there many uses for this fabulous gadget, but it's is easy to use! You can learn more about all the machines Xyron offers by visiting their Web site at www.xyron.com.

affordable, all the way up to die cut systems that are virtually stand-alone computers costing hundreds of dollars.

You can use a button maker for pleasure or profit. I love my button maker, and have used it for fun and fundraising. It is easy to use and, besides buttons, I can make key chains, tags, badges, mirrors, and more.

Craft Kits

You can have all of the craft supplies in the world on hand, but they won't do you much good without the motivation and inspiration required to make the crafts. You can get motivation, inspiration, and even directions for craft projects from books, magazines, and strolling through your favorite craft store, but there is another great way to get inspired—pre-made craft kits! These are available at craft stores, online stores, and even some department stores.

Kits are a great way to buy craft supplies and to try new craft techniques. With a kit you can get all of the supplies needed to try specific crafts, so there is no guesswork or wandering up and down aisles looking for the right products. If you are buying a craft kit for yourself, it will be easy to pick out a kit you want to try. However, what about picking out a kit for someone else? Obviously, you want to make sure you choose something the recipient will enjoy. If you know what kind of crafting they enjoy, such as candle making or beading, then the choice is more obvious. If the person doesn't necessarily have a favorite type of craft, pick something that includes some of their favorite characters, animals, hobbies, etc.

If you are buying a craft kit for a child, the first thing you should do is check the label to see what ages the kit is designed for. Make sure you also check for any warnings on the craft kit's label. Some supplies provided in the kit might be dangerous. Make sure there is nothing included with sharp edges or small parts that may pose

ELSEWHERE ON THE WEB

▶ Take a little time to visit the Making Friends Web site at www.makingfriends.com. This site focuses on crafts for kids, and has a lot of great ideas for scout groups. Not only do they offer a large selection of free craft projects, they also offer all of the supplies to make the crafts. You can also buy individual craft kits or kits for large groups.

choking hazards for young kids. You want to make sure the items in the kit are nontoxic, and check to see if there are any warnings about fumes from glue or paint. There should always be close adult supervision when kids are doing any crafts.

You should also check the label to see what is included in the kit. A craft kit will usually contain everything you need to complete the projects offered, except maybe a basic supply or tool. The companies that create the kits usually assume that people will have the basics at home, such as glue, paint, and scissors. While most people do have those basics lying around, it is nice to read the box and make sure you have everything needed. There is nothing more frustrating than sitting down to complete a craft and not having everything you need to finish it.

Sometimes the cost of buying a kit might not be worth the convenience it provides. You should always weigh the cost of a kit against the cost of purchasing the supplies separately. In a lot of instances, a kit will be the way to go, especially when you're trying a new craft. Buying all of the supplies separately usually costs more—in terms of money and time.

You can also make a note of what is included in various craft kits and make your own! If you purchase all of the supplies separately, you may have enough to make a few identical kits. Find some simple boxes, decorate them, and then add the kit supplies.

Get Linked

The ideas shared here should give you a great start in crafting, and even some fun gadgets to play with, but if you still want more ideas and information about gathering together craft supplies and starting out in crafting, check out these resources on my About.com site.

PICTURES OF CHAPTER I PRODUCTS

Visit this link and find colored photos of all the supplies explained here plus more.

http://about.com/familycrafts/chapter1

CRAFT BOOK PRODUCT REVIEWS

Read my reviews of a large variety of craft products and books.

http://about.com/familycrafts/productreviews

Chapter 2

Make Your Own Craft Supplies

Paint Recipes

You can make your next painting project extra special by mixing your own paint. You can easily make a variety of paint to use in different projects using ingredients you probably have lying around your house. You should make sure you save jars, empty film containers, or pill bottles to store your paint in.

Try mixing up a batch of finger paint, dimensional paint, or even window paint. You can even make your own face paint! A word of warning, though: You should wear a smock or apron not only while painting, but also while mixing these paints, as some of the ingredients may stain clothing. Also, children should always have adult supervision and assistance when working around the stove or any hot ingredients.

Drink Mix Finger Paint

You can use powdered drink mix to create beautiful finger paint. Experiment with all your favorite flavors to see what color paint they make!

1 cup flour	1½ cups water
1 package unsweetened	1½ tablespoons oil
powdered drink mix	Liquid dish soap (optional)
¼ cup salt	

1. In a large bowl, mix together the flour, powdered drink mix, and salt. Put it aside.
2. Measure the water into a medium-sized pot and bring it to a boil. Add the oil to the boiling water.
3. Pour the water and oil mixture into the dry ingredients and mix until they are smooth.
4. Add a few drops of liquid dish soap to your paint mixture and blend carefully so you don't make the mixture bubble. This is optional, but it may help with clean up.
5. Set your paint aside and let it cool before you use it.
6. If the paint is too thick, add more hot water, a little at a time, until it is the consistency you desire.
7. When it is ready to be used, paint on heavy paper.

Flour Finger Paint

You can create a rainbow of colors using this easy recipe that calls for just a few simple ingredients. If you don't have powdered tempera paint, you can try this recipe using food coloring or even a little acrylic paint.

1 cup flour	3 cups water
2 tablespoons of salt	Powdered tempera paint

1. Mix flour and salt together in a large, metal bowl.
2. Pour 1½ cups of the water into a large pot and bring to a boil.
3. While you are waiting for the water to boil, add the other 1½ cups of water to the flour and salt mixture in the metal bowl and stir with a whisk or electric mixer until it is smooth.
4. Once this mixture is smooth, slowly add it to the boiling water, stirring constantly.
5. Boil this mixture until it thickens to the consistency of finger paint. Remove it from the heat and let it cool a little.
6. Decide how many different colors you want, and spoon your paint mixture into a corresponding number of small bowls. Add small amounts of different-colored tempera paint to each bowl until you get the desired colors.

Dimensional Paint

Mix up a batch or two of this paint, and you will be able to add a unique 3D effect to all of your projects.

½ cup salt	¼ to ½ cup water
½ cup flour	Food coloring

1. In a medium-sized bowl, mix together the salt and flour.
2. Start out by adding ¼ cup of water. Stir well.
3. Continue to add water, a few drops at a time, until your mixture is the consistency of a thick milkshake.
4. Add food coloring until your paint is the desired color.
5. To apply your paint, use a small squeeze bottle or spread it onto your project with a craft stick.
6. Let your finished painting dry completely.

WHAT'S HOT

▶ Dimensional paint is very popular and versatile! Besides adding painted designs to fabric, it can be used to embellish any hard surface, such as glass, metal, wood, and plastic. You can add 3D marks and designs that can be used for a tactile activity for kids, or as a tool for someone who has bad eyesight. You can find a variety of projects that use dimensional paint here: http://about.com/family crafts/dpaintcrafts.

Dish Soap Paint

This simple mixture works great for painting temporary designs on windows or even sidewalks. You can also paint on paper—once dry, it looks like a cross between watercolors and oil paints.

> Light-colored liquid dishwashing soap
> Powdered tempera paint

1. In a small bowl, add equal parts of dish soap and powdered tempera paint and mix well.
2. Use a paintbrush to apply this paint. Even though this paint is made using soap, take care to protect clothing and cover the walls, window sills, or any other areas that might get splattered.

Face Paint

This is an easy-to-make paint you can use for face painting at parties or to complement Halloween costumes. Mix up one batch for every color you want to make. When the party is over, the face paint should effortlessly wash off with soap and water. You may want to test this recipe first to make sure there is no staining or irritation.

> 1 teaspoon cornstarch   ½ teaspoon water
> ½ teaspoon cold cream   Powdered tempera paint

1. In a small container, mix together the cornstarch, cold cream, and water.
2. Add the powdered tempera paint a little at a time, stirring well, until you get the desired color.
3. Mix up as many colors as needed and apply with a small paintbrush or a cotton swab.

Glue and Paste Recipes

Use these directions to make a variety of glues using an assortment of ingredients. The kind of glue you will want to make will depend on what kind of project you are doing, so read through them all and choose the one that best suits your needs. Make sure to store any homemade glues and pastes that contain perishable ingredients in airtight containers in the refrigerator.

School Glue

1½ cups water   ½ cup cornstarch
1 teaspoon white vinegar   2 tablespoons light corn syrup

1. Pour ¾ cup of the water into a medium-sized pot along with the corn syrup and vinegar.
2. Bring this mixture to a full boil, stirring often.
3. While you are waiting for that mixture to boil, mix the remaining cold water and the cornstarch together. Beat well to remove all of the lumps.
4. Slowly stir the water and cornstarch into your boiling mixture, stirring constantly.
5. Bring this mixture to a boil and let it boil for 1 minute. Remove the pot from the heat and let cool.
6. Once cooled, put the glue in a covered container and wait at least a day before using.

Cooked Paste

This paste recipe is especially good for paper mache and other paper projects, and it will last for a while if you keep it refrigerated.

> 6 cups water, divided
> 1 cup flour

1. Measure 4 cups of the water into a large pot. Place the pot on the stove and bring the water to a boil.
2. In a large bowl, mix together the flour and the remaining 2 cups of cold water. Stir this mixture well to get out as many lumps as possible.
3. Stir the flour and water mixture slowly into the boiling water, stirring constantly.
4. Simmer for 4 to 5 minutes, stirring occasionally, until mixture is smooth.
5. Remove your paste from the heat and allow it to cool before using it.

No-Cook Paste

This glue is just a simple mixture of flour, water, and salt, but it is usually my first choice when it comes to paper projects. It is quick and gets the job done!

> 1 cup of flour
> 2 cups of water
> 1 teaspoon salt

1. Start out by mixing the flour with 1½ cups of the water. Stir it well to remove as many lumps as possible.

ELSEWHERE ON THE WEB

▶ If you have spent time searching online for crafts for kids, you have probably run across the Kid's Domain Web site (www.kidsdomain.com). It was one of the very first Web sites I frequented in the early days of the World Wide Web. This site now has different owners than it had then, but they still have a large variety of crafts and activities for kids, including a nice collection of craft recipes.

2. Slowly mix in more water until your mixture is the consistency of thick glue.
3. Add the salt and stir well.
4. Use this glue from a squirt bottle or apply with a cotton swab, paintbrush, or a foam brush.

Lick-and-Stick Glue

Make this glue and apply it to the backs of magazine pictures, photocopies, or other pictures, and then let it dry. This recipe gives you enough glue to create dozens of stickers. The glue can be stored in the refrigerator and should be heated to thin it out when you are ready to use it again.

> 1 envelope plain, unflavored gelatin
> 4 tablespoons water
> ½ teaspoon light corn syrup
> ½ teaspoon lemon or peppermint extract
> Pictures from magazines, photocopies, etc.

1. Pour the envelope of gelatin into a small cup with 1 tablespoon of cool water. Let it sit for about 5 minutes.
2. In a small pot, heat the remaining 3 tablespoons of water. Pour in the gelatin water from step 1.
3. Dissolve the gelatin in the boiling water. Remove it from the heat.
4. Add the corn syrup and stir to dissolve, then add the extract of your choice and stir well.
5. Set your glue aside and allow it to cool.
6. Gather together the pictures that you would like to make into stickers or stamps. If your pictures will be cut from larger pieces of paper, it is easiest to cut out the picture after the

WHAT'S HOT

▶ It is very fashionable these days to use colored glue, and you can make your own! Simply pour your glue of choice into a disposable container such as a margarine tub, add a coloring agent, stir with a craft stick or plastic utensil, and then pour it back into the original bottle. For a coloring agent you can use food coloring, powdered drink mix, or powdered tempera paint. For even more of a twist, add a little glitter to your glue.

▶ Yes, you should be cautious, because some products used to add color to your craft-supply recipes might stain. Food coloring, powdered drink mix, and flavored gelatin are some of the homemade craft supplies that can stain clothing, furniture, carpet, and skin, even if they are wiped up right away. Tempera and acrylic paints are less likely to stain fabrics and carpet if cleaned right away.

adhesive has been applied and dried. If you will be coloring your sticker, it is best to color your design with markers after the adhesive has been applied and dried.

7. Once cool enough to touch, use an old paintbrush or a foam brush to apply a thin layer of the glue to the back of your pictures.
8. Let your stickers sit undisturbed until dry. If they curl, simply flatten them once the glue is dry by leaving them under a phone book or other heavy object for a while.
9. To use your stickers, cut out your design, moisten the back by licking it or dabbing it with a damp cloth, and stick it to paper.

Clay Recipes

Whether you want clay to play with or to use for a specific project, one of these recipes should suit your needs. You might be surprised by what you can actually make clay out of. Once your creations have hardened, you can paint them with acrylic or tempera paint and seal them using a clear acrylic sealer.

Bread Clay

You can create miniature sculptures using this dough. Once you have the desired shapes and designs, let them air dry for at least 24 hours. Then you can paint and embellish however you want.

7 pieces of white bread
7 teaspoons white school glue
½ teaspoon liquid dishwashing soap
Water

1. Remove the crusts from the pieces of bread and discard. Tear what remains of the slices of bread into small pieces, and put them in a medium-sized bowl.

2. Add the glue to the bread and mix thoroughly. You may have to knead the mixture with your hands, as it may be too thick for a spoon.
3. Stir in the dishwashing soap and mix or knead until you get a nice clay consistency. If this mixture is too dry, add water a few drops at a time and mix until you get a good consistency.

Sawdust Clay

This is a great clay for making projects, as they can be sanded and painted once they are completely dry.

> 1 cup sawdust
> ½ cup dry wallpaper paste
> Water

1. Blend the sawdust and the dry wallpaper paste together.
2. Slowly add water, about ¼ cup at a time, and stir or knead this mixture until it looks like clay.
3. Once you have your clay made, you can make shapes, designs, and creatures—whatever you want!
4. Let your creations dry in a warm, preferably sunny, spot for at least 24 hours before you attempt to sand or paint them.

Applesauce Cinnamon Clay

These make unique, sweet smelling ornaments if you roll them out and cut shapes using cookie cutters. Poke a hole for hanging using a drinking straw. Great for holiday gift giving!

> 1 cup ground cinnamon
> ¼ cup white school glue

TOOLS YOU NEED

▶ There are clays available to mold and shape that stay soft and are easy to work with. There are clays available that you can use to make sculptures that will set up and harden with heat or without. There are so many kinds of clay—where do you begin? You can learn more about the different kinds of clay available by visiting this page: http://about.com/familycrafts/playwithclay.

½ cup applesauce

1. In a medium-sized bowl, mix all three ingredients together.
2. Knead dough to mix well. If your dough is too dry, add a little more glue; if it is too wet, add a little more cinnamon.
3. Shape as desired, or roll them out like cookie dough.
4. Put your creations in a warm, dry spot to dry. This will take a few days, and if your projects start to curl, simply flip them over.

Dryer-Lint Clay

Start saving that dryer lint now, and then mix up a batch of clay later. Not only will you make some unique clay, this is an exceptional way to recycle.

2 cups dryer lint (lightly packed)
⅓ cup white glue
1 tablespoon dishwashing soap
¼ to ⅓ cup warm water

1. Measure the dryer lint into a bowl and rip it into small pieces.
2. Pour in the white glue, dishwashing soap, and ¼ cup of the water.
3. Mix this all together, kneading if necessary. If the mixture is too dry, you can add more water, a teaspoon at a time, until your lint dough is easy to work with.
4. Store your clay covered to keep it moist, or let it sit out to air dry for several days.

Cooked Play Clay

Once cooled, this dough is easy to handle and can be played with for hours of entertainment. It can be stored in plastic bags or shaped into interesting projects and dried (this clay dries to a very hard finish).

> 2 cups baking soda
> 1 cup cornstarch
> 1¼ cup water

1. Mix all three ingredients together in a medium pot.
2. Bring the mixture to a boil, stirring often, and cook it over medium heat until it resembles mashed potatoes.
3. Pour the mixture into a bowl, cover it with a damp cloth, and let it cool.
4. You can play with the clay as soon as it is cool enough to handle.

No-Cook Play Clay

While you can make this clay without using the stove, you can use the oven to help dry your finished pieces. Set the oven to about 250°F and place your finished clay pieces inside it until they are dry. This usually takes at least an hour, but the time will vary depending on the size of your projects.

> 2 cups flour
> 1 cup salt
> 2 tablespoons vegetable oil
> ¾ to 1 cup water

WHAT'S HOT

▶ It seems like just about any clay recipe you find can either be cooked or not. So, what is the correct way to do it? I have concluded through extensive research and experimentation that either way works. I know this is not very helpful, but it should encourage you to spend more time together making clay to see which way you prefer. More recipes you can experiment with can be found here: http://about.com/familycrafts/clayrecipes.

1. In a large bowl, mix together flour and salt.
2. Add the oil and about ¾ cup of water. Stir or knead it to mix well.
3. If your clay is too dry, add more water, a little at a time. If your mixture gets too wet, add more flour, a little at a time.

More Creative Recipes

There are plenty of other creative recipes you can make. Take some time and make your own sidewalk chalk or bubbles and wands, and take them outside and have some fun. For some indoor amusement, you can make your own crayons and paper.

Sidewalk Chalk

When working with plaster of Paris, it is best to use disposable containers and utensils. If you do use your own household bowls and spoons, do not wash them in a sink where the plaster of Paris powder can wash down the drain. You should rinse them off outside using a hose. Your finished chalk may take a few days to dry, so plan accordingly.

> 1 cup plaster of Paris
> ¾ cup water
> Tempera paint
> Molds

1. Combine the plaster of Paris and water in a bowl and mix well.
2. Add the tempera paint, a few drops at a time, and stir until you get the desired color (you can also leave your chalk white if you prefer).

▶ There are a variety of household items you can use as molds when you make sidewalk chalk. My favorite molds to use are small paper cups like those used in bathroom dispensers. You can also use toilet-tissue rolls, candy molds, cookie cutters, lined muffin tins, ice-cube trays, or any other small container. Most of these molds can also be used for making crayons; just make sure your mold is heat resistant, and you may want to line it with foil.

3. Once you are done adding paint, if your mixture seems too watery, add a little more plaster of Paris, a teaspoon at a time.
4. Pour your chalk mixture into your molds. Let dry undisturbed for about 24 hours.
5. Remove your chalk from the mold. For larger molds, or if your chalk feels damp, you should let your chalk dry for another 24 hours before you use it.

Sidewalk Paint

You've probably heard of sidewalk chalk, but how about sidewalk paint? Let the kids mix up a batch of this paint and spend time outside painting the sidewalk red!

½ cup water
½ cup cornstarch
Food coloring
Jar with lid
Paintbrushes, foam brushes, and/or
    sponges

1. Measure the water, cornstarch, and food coloring into a jar.
2. Replace the lid, screwing on tightly. Shake the jar until the paint is completely mixed.
3. Repeat the first two steps for every color you want to make.
4. Paint roads, games, and even huge murals on your sidewalk. You can also make fun shapes using sponges. If the paint gets a little too dry, simply add a little bit of water.
5. When you are done playing, this environmentally friendly sidewalk paint can be washed off using a hose.

Homemade Blowing Bubbles

Use this recipe and you can blow bubbles for days. Try blowing bubbles using slotted spoons, chenille stems formed into interesting shapes, loops made out of wire hangers, or even your hands formed in the shape of a circle! If you have trouble with bugs, such as bees, being attracted to this sweet formula, try substituting glycerin for the corn syrup. (Glycerin is inexpensive, safe to use with kids, and can be found in most drug stores.)

> 2 cups water
> 2 tablespoons light corn syrup
> ½ cup hand dishwashing soap

1. Mix together the water and the corn syrup. Stir quickly until they are well blended.
2. Add the dishwashing soap and stir slowly. You want to try to avoid making the mixture bubble, as this may weaken your bubbles.
3. While this mixture can be used to blow bubbles right away, for best results, pour this mixture into a clean jar or plastic container, cover, and let sit in the refrigerator overnight.

Recycled Crayons

Here is a fun activity you can do to recycle old, broken crayons. You can transform them into new crayons using this technique and the mold of your choice. For a mold, you can use anything that will hold the hot wax as it cools. You can make rainbow crayons by using pieces of several different colored crayons, or make single colored crayons.

> Broken crayons
> Tin can
> Molds

ELSEWHERE ON THE WEB

▶ If you are interested in blowing bubbles, you might want to check out the Bubblesphere Web site at www.bubbles.org. This is an extensive site with more information than you ever wanted to know about bubbles. Besides reading the history of bubbles and FAQs about bubbles, you can play unique online games and talk to others in the forum. You can also explore new bubble-solution recipes.

1. Put a small pot with a couple of inches of water in it on the stove. Heat the water to a gentle boil, then simmer.
2. Remove any paper from the crayons. Break the crayons into pieces as small as you can and put them in the tin can (any paper labels should be removed from can). The number of crayons you use will depend on the size of your mold.
3. Place the tin can of crayons in the pot of hot water until they melt.
4. Once melted, remove the tin can from the pot using an oven mitt.
5. Carefully pour the hot wax into your mold, and set it aside to cool.
6. Once the wax is cooled and set, pop your crayons out of the mold and use!

Make Your Own Paper

Believe it or not, it is not too hard to make your own paper. Start out making basic sheets of paper to test it out, and then experiment with adding color, spices, seeds, and much more. Experiment with pieces of pictures from magazines, newsprint, construction paper, uncoated wrapping paper, and other colored paper. You are only limited by your imagination!

Newspaper
Old paper
Water
2 teaspoons liquid starch
Piece of window screen, about 10" × 12"
    (found at the hardware store)
Unwanted 8" × 10" frame
Stapler

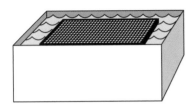

Blender
Plastic tub (large enough to submerge the frame in)
Sponge or lint-free cloth
White felt—8" × 12" sheets work well (you need 1 piece for
    each sheet of paper you will make)

1. Cover your work surface with newspaper. (For added protection you can lay down newspaper on top of wax paper.)
2. Rip your chosen paper into small pieces, about 1" square. Mix and match to create your own unique paper. Start out by ripping up about 5 cups (gently packed) of paper.
3. Put your ripped paper and about 3 cups of water in a bowl and let it soak. The longer it soaks, the easier it will blend.
4. Fill your plastic tub ⅓ of the way full with water and set it on your covered work surface.
5. Make a paper screen (also called a mold) by removing the back and glass from the frame and stapling the piece of screen on the back of the frame. Make sure the screen is pulled as tightly as possible.
6. Pour ⅓ of your paper and water mixture into the blender. Add 1 cup of water, or as much as will fit. Blend until smooth.
7. Pour the blended mixture into the plastic tub that you put water in earlier.
8. Blend two more batches of the paper and water mixture as you did the first, and pour them into the plastic tub.
9. Add the liquid starch (this step is optional; however, the starch acts as sizing which will help stop any ink used on this paper from bleeding). Stir this mixture well.
10. Immediately take your framed screen and submerge it in your plastic bin with the stapled side up. Slowly lift the screen, wiggling it gently side-to-side to help distribute the paper mixture evenly.
11. Dip and lift your screen until you have an even, thin layer of paper on it. The thinner your paper layer is, the better.

12. Hold the screen over the tub until the water is done dripping.

13. If you want to add embellishments to your paper, do it now.

14. Set your frame, paper-side-up, on your work surface. Lay a sheet of felt over the paper, making sure to cover it all. Hold the edges of the felt tight and flip your paper over. The felt should now be lying on your work surface with your piece of paper and the screen on top of that.

15. Using the sponge or lint-free cloth, pat the screen side of the paper, removing as much water as possible. Wring out the sponge or cloth if necessary. Keep patting (do not rub) your paper piece until you can see it start separating from the screen.

16. Now, hold down one corner of the felt square and gently lift the corner of your frame. With any luck, your newly made piece of paper should pull away from the frame, staying on the piece of felt. If your piece of paper does not pull cleanly away from the screen, or if it breaks, simply put it back in the tub with your paper and water mixture and try again.

17. Leave your paper on the sheet of felt and set it aside to dry (usually overnight).

18. Stir your paper pulp mixture and then repeat steps 10 through 17 for each sheet of paper you want to make. This recipe should get you about six pieces of paper, but that amount will vary depending on the thickness of your paper.

19. Once the paper is dry to the touch, carefully peel it away from the felt. If the felt side is still wet, lay it damp-side-up and let it dry completely.

20. When all of your paper is completely dry, stack them on top of each other and then place heavy books on top to flatten them. You can also try ironing them using a pressing cloth and an iron set on medium heat.

21. Use a paper trimmer or scissors to square up your paper's edges, and your new paper is now ready to use!

Get Linked

You do not have to spend a fortune on paint, glue, and other craft supplies—you can try making your own. Not only is the finished product useful, but the process is fun for both kids and adults! Use these resources to make even more craft supplies:

CRAFT SUPPLY RECIPES

Find even more fun recipes for making your own craft supplies.
http://about.com/familycrafts/myosupplies

CREATIVE SNACK IDEAS

Use your imagination and these creative recipes to make fun snacks.
http://about.com/familycrafts/creativesnacks

Chapter 3

Crafting Techniques

The Art of Decoupage

Decoupage is the art of embellishing an object with pictures cut from various sources, such as magazines, wrapping paper, and napkins. The pictures are glued onto the object and then covered by a glasslike finish to cover, seal, and protect them. The term comes from the old French word decouper, meaning "to cut out." It was traditionally used to decorate boxes, screens, panels, and furniture.

Looking at the finished product, you might think decoupage is complicated, but it is actually quite simple! If you can cut and paste, you already know most of the techniques involved. I think sometimes the hardest part of decoupage is taking your time and having patience while you wait for the glue and/or decoupage medium to dry. If you take your time while making your decoupage project, however, your finished product can be so stunning that it can appear to be professionally painted.

All kinds of surfaces can be decoupaged. You can use this craft technique to decorate glass, wood, tin, paper mache, ceramics, soap, candles, terra cotta, and just about anything else you can think of. Decoupage is a wonderful way to personalize a picture frame, dress up a drab mirror, or refinish battered furniture. There's almost nothing you can't beautify with a little bit of paper, glue, and patience!

You can purchase supplies and tools that are made specifically for decoupage. The supplies aren't too expensive, and include decoupage medium, specialty papers/pictures, and a brayer or rubber squeegee. One of the nice things about this craft, however, is that you can also use supplies that you probably already have in the house. You can make your own decoupage medium, use pictures from magazines or wrapping paper, and use a damp sponge in place of a brayer/squeegee.

The first thing you need when it comes to decoupage is the object you want to decorate. As mentioned previously, this can be just about anything. A smooth surface is preferable, and your item should be free of dust and dirt. For your first project, you may want to experiment on a scrap piece of wood or another object that you don't really care about.

If you are interested in buying specialized decoupage tools and supplies, add these to your shopping list:

- **Decoupage papers:** You can buy coordinating pictures or packs of paper to use for decoupage projects.
- **Decoupage medium:** You can find a variety of brands in any craft store. It is used to glue the picture to your item and seal it.
- **Foam or small paintbrush:** Used to apply and spread decoupage medium and/or sealer.

- **Craft knife:** Looks and is held like a pencil. It is used to cut out detailed pictures.
- **Cutting mat:** For use with the craft knife.
- **Brayer:** This is like a miniature rolling pin, designed to help remove wrinkles and air bubbles, remove excess glue, and stick your picture down better.
- **Rubber squeegee:** A small squeegee used for the same reason you would use a brayer.
- **Sealer:** This is your project's final coat. You can use your decoupage medium or glue as a sealer, or you can use polyurethane, acrylic spray, or whatever sealer you prefer to use.

While the specialty tools might make your crafting go a little smoother, for most of the above products, you can use items you may already have:

- **Decoupage pictures:** You can use pictures from magazines or catalogs, wrapping paper, or photocopied computer printouts or photographs.
- **Scissors:** Used to cut out pictures.
- **White school glue:** Use this as your decoupage medium. You can glue your pictures down and seal them. To seal, I prefer to dilute my glue with a bit of water.
- **Cotton swab:** Used to apply and spread glue and/or decoupage medium.
- **Fingers or damp sponge:** These can be carefully used to help remove wrinkles and air bubbles and wipe up excess glue.

There are still a few more things you may want to gather before you start your project:

TOOLS YOU NEED

▶ When you are working on decoupage projects, one of the challenges you face might be to find that perfect picture. If this is the case, then your best bet might be to buy a kit. This can save you a lot of searching, because you will usually get several coordinating designs to help complete your projects. Along with a wide variety of pictures and decorative papers, most of these kits contain basic instructions: http://about.com/familycrafts/deckits.

▶ Mod Podge, made by Plaid, is one of the most popular decoupage medium brands. In fact, years ago the terms decoupage and Mod Podge were interchanged with each other by some. It is usually the decoupage medium I reach for when I am shopping. You have many options, including Mod Podge for outdoor projects, for fabric projects, and for walls. There are also three different finishes: gloss, matte, and sparkle. Learn more at www .modpodge.com.

- **Sandpaper:** To remove any rough patches from the object you will be decoupaging.
- **Paint:** Can be used as a base coat for the object you will be decoupaging.
- **Tweezers:** To help apply smaller pictures.
- **Wax paper or parchment paper:** Lay this down on your work surface to protect it from paint, glue, or decoupage-medium spills.
- **Damp rag:** To wipe up spills and excess glue.

Directions are there for a reason! As with any craft project, you should read through all of the directions before you begin. These are basic step-by-step directions. As you get more confident you can try different things, such as decoupaging around corners or dimensional decoupage.

1. Prepare the item you will be decoupaging the pictures onto. The item should have a smooth, clean surface—sand and wash it if necessary. It can be sealed or painted if you desire.
2. Choose and prepare the pictures you will be decoupaging onto your project. You can use coordinating decoupage papers, magazine pictures, or motifs cut from wrapping paper. Bigger designs can be cut with scissors; more detailed pictures can be cut out using a craft knife. Figure out the picture placements on your item.
3. Working with one picture at a time, cover the back of a picture with glue or decoupage medium. Position the picture onto the surface of your item, and carefully press with fingers, damp sponge, brayer, or rubber squeegee to work out air bubbles or wrinkles. For a large picture,

start from the center and work your way out. Remove any excess glue with a damp cloth or sponge. Once all pictures are applied, let the glue dry completely.

4. Now you need to apply your decoupage finish. Use the decoupage medium (or slightly diluted white glue) to coat your item entirely. Let this coat dry completely.

5. Apply a second coat of decoupage medium (or diluted glue) and let it dry completely. Keep applying coats of decoupage medium until you can run your hand over the surface and not feel the edge of the paper, or until you have the effect you want. Make sure you allow each coat to dry completely before applying another coat.

6. If desired, you can use a polyurethane or acrylic spray sealer as your final coat, but this is not necessary.

Your decoupaged project is now done! Though decoupaging projects do take a while to complete, the process is easy enough for anyone to do. You can use the directions here to make a large variety of projects, including matching home decor or unique gifts.

How to Paper Mache

The term paper mache, French for "chewed-up paper," is used to describe the process of using pieces of paper and a wet paste to make crafts. The most popular items made using this technique are piñatas, boxes, and fruit shapes. Using paper-mache techniques, you can create almost anything. Paper mache is one of the most versatile crafts around, and there is no right or wrong way to do it. The best part is that you probably already have everything you need to create paper-mache masterpieces.

The steps you follow to make paper-mache crafts are easy. The only drawback is that, similar to decoupage, paper-mache projects sometimes take a long time to finish, simply because they are made

ASK YOUR GUIDE

Can I use photographs or computer printouts in my decoupage projects?

▶ Your best bet when it comes to using photographs or designs printed at home is to get colored photocopies made and use those. You don't want to use pictures from your home printer because that ink will run when it gets wet from the glue or decoupage medium. Also, using photographs is a challenge because the thick photo paper takes forever to dry and has a tendency to bubble.

with several layers and each layer needs to dry before the next one is applied. Some creations can take several days to finish, so be prepared and be patient!

Paper mache is fairly simple. To create wonderful paper-mache crafts, you really only need three things: paper, a mold or form, and paste. You should be able to either find these things around your house, or make them from items you have. For more detailed work, you can mix up a batch of paper-mache pulp.

- **Paper:** The best paper to use for paper mache is old news-paper. The sheets are thin enough to soak up the paste nicely, and they blend together easier to make a smoother finished product. If you are worried about the printing on the paper or want a more natural finish, you can make the last paper-mache layer out of white paper or paper towels. If you use brown paper towels for the last layer or two, you can get a nice leather or rustic look without finishing!
- **Mold or form:** You can use many items found around your house to make molds and forms for your paper-mache projects. Here are some suggestions for items to use. Some can be used as bases for the projects, while others can be used to add specific details such as arms and legs. Masking tape can be used for holding different forms together while you apply the paper-mache paste and newspaper.

1. **Balloons:** All sizes and shapes make great bases for rounded designs or piñatas.
2. **Cardboard:** Corrugated cardboard makes sturdy bases, while lightweight cardboard, like cereal boxes, works well for details.

▶ One of the most popular crafts made using paper-mache techniques is a piñata, a hollow paper-mache cre-ation that is filled with treats and small prizes and then suspended from a high place. Partygoers then take turns trying to break open the piñata by hitting it while blind-folded. Pick out a theme for your party and make a match-ing piñata, or find a design here: http://about.com/family crafts/makeapinata.

3. **Newspaper:** Besides being a key ingredient in holding your paper-mache creation together, you can use it for creating details. Try rolling it to make an arm or leg, or ball it up to make smaller parts.

4. **Shoe boxes:** Cover with paper mache to make a fancy box, or use as a base for a bigger project.

5. **Toilet tissue and paper-towel rolls:** Great for adding details like arms and legs.

6. **Chicken wire:** Use this as a base for large projects.

This list can be endless. If you have it lying around your house, you can probably use it as a mold for your paper-mache projects!

Paste

You can easily mix up a batch of paste to use with your paper-mache crafts. There are many different recipes available, and no single paste recipe is better than another. Experiment and use the paste you prefer the most, or the one that works best for your current project. If working with younger children, I would use one of the flour recipes just in case they get the mixture on their fingers and stick them in their mouths. If covered tightly, the paste can be stored for several days. The first two recipes should be stored in the refrigerator.

1. This is usually my first choice. Use a simple mixture of flour and water. Mix one part flour with about two parts water, until you get a consistency like thick glue. Add more water or flour as necessary. Mix well to get out all of the bumps. You can add a few tablespoons of salt to help prevent mold.

2. Put 4 cups of water into a large pot and bring it to a boil on the stove. While you are waiting for the water to boil, mix together 1 cup of flour with 1 cup of water, stirring well to get

TOOLS YOU NEED

▶ **If you want an instant paper-mache pulp, you can try Celluclay** (http://store .artcity.com/howto-celluclay .html)**. It is a finely textured, non-toxic material that handles like clay, and it can be used like paper-mache pulp. Celluclay can be molded into any shape and adheres to almost any surface. The dried forms can be sawed, sanded, nailed, or waterproofed. You can paint or seal the finished product like you would any paper-mache product.**

out as many bumps as possible. Carefully add your flour and water mixture to the boiling water, stirring constantly. Simmer this mixture for 2 to 3 minutes, until smooth. Add a few table-spoons of salt to help prevent mold. Allow to cool before you try to use it.

3. You can use regular glue mixed with a bit of water. Mix using about one part water to two parts glue.

4. Use wallpaper paste. Follow the directions from the manufac-turer to mix, except use a little less water. If the mixture is too thick, add more water a little at a time. This may work better in more humid climates.

5. Use liquid starch, as is.

Paper-mache Pulp

A pulp mixture is great for making smooth, fine details in your paper-mache creations, or for creating small objects. It would, however, take a lot of it to complete a larger project. All you need to make this special mixture is newspaper, water, salt, and glue.

1. Start out by tearing the newspaper into tiny pieces and putting them in a large bowl. Add just enough warm-to-hot water to completely cover the newspaper. Let it soak for several hours or overnight.

2. Once your newspaper has soaked for several hours, get your hands into it! Play with it, mix it, and squeeze it through your fingers until it looks like oatmeal. Try to get as many lumps out as possible. If necessary, add a bit more water and let it soak a little more.

3. Once you have it as smooth as possible, add a few tablespoons of salt to help retard mold.

4. Mix it again with your hands. Once mixed thoroughly, squeeze out any excess water and add a few tablespoons of glue.
5. Store your pulp in an airtight baggie or bowl in the refrigerator for a very long time!

The objects you can make with paper mache are only limited by your imagination. So, use your imagination and let's get started!

1. Paper mache is a very messy craft, so start out by covering your work surface, or you can even do it outside if weather permits. Make sure you cover yourself also.
2. Use the suggestions above to create the mold or form you will paper mache.
3. Once your mold is ready, prepare a good supply of newspaper by tearing it into small strips, about 1" × 4" Always tear your newspaper into strips instead of cutting them. Torn paper lays better on paper-mache creations and makes for smoother edges.
4. Choose a paste recipe and prepare it as directed. Pour it into a bowl.
5. When your paste is ready, start out by dipping one piece of paper in the paste. Hold the strip over the paste bowl and run it through your fingers to squeeze off excess paste. The strip should be completely saturated.
6. Stick the newspaper strip over the form you want to paper mache, and smooth it down with your fingers.
7. Repeat steps 5 and 6 until your entire form is covered. The newspaper pieces should overlap each other. It may take several hours to complete one layer, because you may have to wait for one side to dry enough to flip it over and finish the other side.
8. After one layer is complete, let it dry for about 24 hours.

◀ Balloon being covered with newspaper using paper mache techniques

▶ You can use almost anything as your tesserae when you are making mosaics. As mentioned here, typical objects used are small tiles, marbles, tumbled glass pieces, or pottery fragments. Other objects you might consider are polished stones, small mirrors, beads, or buttons. Look through your junk drawers at home to see what else you can add to your stepping stones—olds keys, useless coins, sea shells, or broken CDs.

9. Add another layer of newspaper strips and let dry for another 24 hours.
10. Repeat this process until you get the desired effect, but you should have at least three layers.

If your project needs finer details or if you need to smooth around your forms, you can use the paper-mache pulp. Experiment with your forms, paste, and pulp until you are satisfied with your finished project. Once completed and dry, your final product can be painted, decoupaged, or decorated any way you want.

Making Mosaics

Mosaics are pictures made by arranging small colorful objects (also called tesserae) into fancy designs on top of a base. You set them into a grout or other adhesive, and then usually apply grout around them to secure them in place. The tesserae used will vary, but they are usually small pieces of colored marble, glass, pottery fragments, or tile. With them, you can make stunning furniture or create abstract pieces of art.

This craft is easy to learn and to get started, and can be enjoyed by all ages with the proper supervision. It can also be taken to advanced levels. Start out small and with basic supplies and work your way up from there.

You need a few different tools and supplies to make a mosaic.   No matter how fancy or simple you want your mosaic to be, there are four main supplies you need to make a mosaic masterpiece:

- **A base:** This is the item you will make the mosaic on, like a tabletop, stepping stone, or piece of plywood. It can be anything with a flat, hard surface.
- **Tessarae:** As I said previously, your tessarae are the small items you use to make your mosaic design. Traditionally, these are colored marbles, glass pieces, pottery fragments, or small tiles. You can, however, use anything that strikes your fancy.
- **Adhesive:** This is what attaches the tessarae to the base. Depending on the method you choose, this can be either a mosaic glue or grout.
- **Grout:** This is a cement-like mixture used to fill the gaps between the tessarae in a mosaic project. It can also be used as the adhesive.

The easiest way to try out this craft is to purchase tessarae. Most craft stores sell a large selection of objects in a variety of shapes, sizes, and colors that can be used as-is. If you want to use items you have laying around your house, you may need a few tools:

- **Tile cutter:** It is used for cutting down larger ceramic tiles.
- **Glass cutter:** This is used to cut down large pieces of glass.

ELSEWHERE ON THE WEB

▶ When you have a few minutes, sit at your computer and visit the Mosaic Tile Guide (www.mosaic-tile-guide.com). Yes, there are wonderful, educational articles that teach you such things as how to cut tiles, how to apply grout, and how to mix color, but check out all of the wonderful pictures! The photographs in this site's gallery are amazing. If these photos don't inspire you, I don't know what will!

- **Nippers:** This tool is used for cleanly breaking small pieces off of tile, or sometimes glass tessarae.
- **Hammer:** A hammer can be used to break up pottery, china, CDs, and other items you can use in mosaics. The object to be hit with the hammer should be wrapped in an old towel so pieces do not fly around.

Of course, there are some basic crafting and safety supplies you will need. You should have these things lying around your house:

- **Work gloves:** To protect your hands while breaking apart tessarae.
- **Safety glasses:** To protect your eyes while breaking apart tessarae.
- **Latex gloves:** The use of these is optional; they can be used when handling grout.
- **Dust mask:** This can be worn to protect yourself when working with the grout in powdered form.
- **Wax paper and newspaper:** Use these items to cover your work surface as this is a very messy craft!
- **Stir stick:** A paint stir stick works great for mixing grout.
- **Bucket:** I use an old ice cream bucket for mixing the grout in.
- **Kitchen spatula:** Use this tool, or something similar, to spread the grout onto your mosaic.
- **Clean rags and/or sponges:** To wipe grout off of tile surface after applying.

The final thing you will need before you start making your mosaic is a pattern. You can purchase a pattern, draw your own, or simply create an abstract pattern as you go.

There are two ways to make your mosaic: the grout method and the glue method. The one you choose may depend on the pattern you are using. Read through the directions for each method and decide which will work best for you.

Example of a mosaic pattern

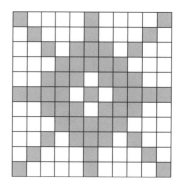

You can use the grout method to make a mosaic. While many of the steps are the same no matter which method you use, when using the grout method for making a mosaic, grout is applied to the base and the tessarae are gently pushed into the grout mixture.

1. Make sure your base is free of dust and dirt. If your base has a smooth surface, you may want to run some sandpaper over it to give the grout a porous surface to stick to.
2. Mix up the grout by following the directions on the package.
3. Spread the grout evenly over your base. I would suggest you make it about ½" thick.
4. Lay your tessarae, right side up, onto the grout, pushing gently to embed. The grout will come up around the outer edges of the tessarae to secure it in place. You will see the grout between the pieces as you lay them down.
5. Let your project dry for several hours or overnight.
6. Once dry, use a damp sponge or rag to clean your mosaic, and it is now ready to use! If your mosaic will be used often or placed outside, make sure you use a grout sealer.

The glue method is the way to go if you have a written pattern to follow. If you use the glue method for making your mosaic, your pattern is traced onto the base and glue is applied to each piece of tessarae, which is then stuck to the appropriate section of the pattern.

1. Make sure your base is free of dust and dirt. If your base has a smooth surface, you may want to run some sandpaper over it to give the glue a porous surface to stick to.
2. Draw your design onto your base. You can either draw it freehand or using carbon tracing paper.
3. Apply your tessarae to the pattern, one piece at a time, by coating the back of the tessarae with a mosaic adhesive (check your local craft store) and sticking them in place on the base.
4. Continue to glue and stick your tessarae, leaving small gaps in between pieces, until your base is covered.
5. Let your project dry for several hours or overnight.
6. Once the glue is dry, mix up a batch of grout and spread it over the top of your project to fill the gaps between the tessarae. You can use a rubber spatula or similar tool to spread the grout and remove any excess.
7. Immediately use a damp sponge or rag to wipe the excess grout off of the tessarae. Get off as much grout as possible without removing any from between the tessarae.
8. Let your project dry for several hours or overnight.
9. Once dry, use a damp sponge or rag to clean your mosaic, and it is now ready to use! If your mosaic will be used often or placed outside, make sure you use a grout sealer.

All about Beading

There are not many kids or even adults who can resist the allure of beads. The list of crafts you can make using beads and a few other supplies is very long. While we can't cover them all here, we can cover the basic supplies for beading and the different kinds of beads.

When it comes to working with beads, you need two things: beads and something to string the beads onto. Even the fanciest beaded jewelry only uses these two supplies. It is the beading technique used that, for the most part, determines how elegant the finished product looks.

You can find beads made of plastic, glass, wood, metal, and even stone. These beads come in a variety of shapes, colors, and sizes, and I could fill half a book just talking about all of those varieties. Instead, I will talk about the beads more commonly used when working with kids.

In many of the projects that kids enjoy working on, you will find pony beads, E beads, or seed beads. Pony beads are larger beads, which makes them great for kids to use to make their own jewelry. Pony beads are often made out of plastic. Also popular is what are known as E beads, which are pretty much identical to pony beads, just smaller. You can find a large selection of these made of plastic or glass. Finally, there are seed beads. These are shaped similar to a pony bead, but they are much smaller than even E beads. These are also readily available in either glass or plastic.

The most important thing to know when it comes to beads is the sizes. Bead sizes are determined by the number of beads per inch. For example, a common size for seed beads is 11/0. That means approximately eleven of them strung together would measure about 1". A common size for E beads is 6/0, and the most common size for pony beads is 3/0. The higher the number, the smaller the bead.

Keeping these tips in mind will better help you choose beads for your project than knowing fancy names and technical terms. The most important thing to keep in mind when buying beads

WHAT'S HOT

▶ Did you know you can create popular jewelry using beads and safety pins? All you have to do is slip some seed beads onto small safety pins, slip the small beaded pins onto a larger pin, and you have created fun items to wear, share, and swap! They make great gifts, too. Check out this page to find step-by-step instructions, free patterns, and more: http://about.com/familycrafts/beadsafetypins.

is simply to buy what you like. There are so many special shapes and styles available you will have fun shopping, experimenting, and beading.

There are many products available for stringing your beads. The one you choose will depend on your budget, the size of the beads you are working with, and the project you are making. Here is a list of the more popular products available:

- **Cord:** This is available in a variety of styles and materials such as satin, leather, elastic, and cotton. Our favorite is the transparent stretch cord.
- **Hemp:** This is commonly used with beads and macramé techniques to create your masterpieces using knots.
- **Thread:** Embroidery thread can be used like hemp. You can also use metallic thread or elastic thread to make jewelry.
- **Ribbon:** Use ¼"-thick ribbon to make fun jewelry, or for one of my top choices—making pony bead creatures.
- **Plastic lacing:** This is commonly used when making pony bead creatures. However, it is hard to tie tightly.
- **Wire:** You can find a large selection of soft, colorful craft wire on the market, or you can try a product called Memory Wire, which is a hard, strong wire that remembers its original shape after being stretched.
- **Monofilament:** You can use this plain fishing line for an invisible string effect.
- **Yarn:** Simple yarn can be used in your beading projects. To make it easier to thread, wrap the end with tape.
- **Safety pins:** One of the more popular sections on my Web site explains how to make jewelry using beads and safety pins.

Of course, you may need a few other supplies to help you with your beading projects. Graph paper is a nice tool to have on hand when it comes to designing original pony bead creatures or jewelry. Tweezers and needle-nosed pliers are helpful when it comes to handling and positioning small beads. You might want to keep a selection of jewelry supplies on hand, along with key rings, zipper pulls, and other items to help make your beaded creations useful.

ELSEWHERE ON THE WEB

▶ I really enjoyed reading through all of the pages on the Beadage Web site (www .beadage.net). The beading glossary and beading-supply tutorial they offer are very informative, and the project ideas shared, complete with color photographs, are wonderful. I also took some time to visit all of the beading-supply resources listed (the author highlighted her favorite purchases), and browsed through all of the amazing photographs shared in the gallery.

Get Linked

This chapter teaches you the basics of some of the more popular crafts out there, but there are so many more techniques you can explore. Use the resources offered here to discover more crafts you might enjoy.

CRAFT TECHNIQUES 101

If you are new to crafting or just want to learn how to do a new technique or use a specific medium, check out these educational how-to's and tutorials.

http://about.com/familycrafts/techniques

CRAFTING TIPS

Browse through many great craft-related tips and tricks, many shared by experienced crafters.

http://about.com/familycrafts/craftingtips

Chapter 4

Child Development and Crafting

Crafts for Toddlers and Preschoolers

Although toddlers and preschoolers do not have the coordination or patience for involved projects, they do love arts and crafts. Most like working with clay, stickers, crayons, and paint—and they also love working with you! At this age, crafts can help kids start to develop both fine-motor skills and cognitive skills.

You will want to introduce them to different craft materials and give them guidance in using those materials, instead of planning specific craft projects. With younger kids, I would suggest focusing much more on the process of the craft activity and not worrying about the finished product.

There are a few safety guidelines you should keep in mind when crafting with toddlers and preschoolers. First of all, the scissors this age group should be introduced to should have plastic blades and a rounded tip. Read labels—all supplies, such as paint, glue, and clay

About

should be nontoxic. You should also pay close attention to the size of the supplies you provide, because many kids in this age group still like to put everything in their mouths!

You will be amazed by how enthusiastic and creative they can be once you start introducing them to various craft items. Check out the following projects.

Cereal Jewelry

This is a fun activity that can also be used for snack time. Just let the kids keep threading the cereal onto the chenille stems until they get bored, and then they can eat them!

Cereal with a hole in the center (Cheerios, Fruit Loops, etc.)
Chenille stems

1. Set out a pile of chenille stems and bowls full of different cereals.
2. Curl up one end of the chenille stem.
3. Show your child how to thread the cereal onto the chenille stem.
4. Let her fill up as many or as few chenille stems as she wants.
5. Once a chenille stem is full (or full enough to fit around the child's wrist), twist both ends together and she can slip it on her wrist.
6. Attach two or three chenille stems together to form a necklace, or, if she likes, you can leave the chenille stem straight.

Contact-Paper Collage

This is a great collage project without any of the gluey mess. For collage items that cannot be cut by safety scissors or torn by hand, cut them into small scrap pieces ahead of time for your child to use.

WHAT'S HOT

▶ Crafts and activities related to preserving memories are very popular. However, sometimes we don't take a few extra moments to do that with our kids' artwork. Every time your child makes an arts and crafts project, take a few moments to write the date and any other important information on the back of the project. Believe me, years later you will be happy you did!

Clear contact paper

Flat collage items (construction paper, tissue paper, crepe paper, magazines, feathers, wrapping paper, etc.)

Colored masking tape

1. Cut two pieces of contact paper the same size.
2. Pull the backing off one of the pieces and lay it on the work surface, sticky-side-up. Tape the corners down to hold it in place.
3. Encourage your child to touch the sticky contact paper to see what it feels like. Show her how to make a collage by sticking small pieces cut or torn from any or all of the collage items onto the contact paper.
4. When she's done adding items to the collage, take the piece of paper off of the back of the other piece of contact paper and carefully lay it over the top of the collage, sticky-side-down. You want all of the collage items sandwiched between the two pieces of contact paper.
5. Add a "frame" to your collage by folding pieces of colored masking tape around the edges.

Rattle Bottle

Kids won't just enjoy assembling this rattle, they'll also enjoy playing with it after it's made.

Clear, plastic water bottle (16 ounces or smaller)	Funnel
	Rice
Small trinkets (beads, buttons, plastic gems, charms, etc.)	Glue

1. Make sure the water bottle is clean and dry and remove any labels.

What are open-ended arts and crafts projects?

▶ Open-ended projects follow the belief that the process of doing a project is more important than what the finished product looks like. Have you noticed that young children usually don't care what their finished product looks like? That is because their focus is on what they are doing, like the clay squishing through their fingers or the way different colors of paint are swirling together.

2. Place a funnel in the bottle. Have your child scoop up rice using a tablespoon and pour it into the funnel.
3. Continue this until he grows bored or until the bottle is about ¼ of the way full. Then let him choose trinkets to put in the bottle. Encourage him to count as he drops the items in, or have him tell you the color of each trinket.
4. Once he is happy with the trinkets added, put a few dabs of glue around the top threads and screw on the cap tightly. After a few minutes of drying time, the rattle is ready for use!

Crafts for PreK and Kindergarten

This age group is working on mastering fine-motor skills like cutting and writing. With practice, they can cut straight lines and write their names. They try to draw pictures of themselves, family members, and other familiar objects. They are also working on learning and memorizing important things they need to know for kindergarten, like numbers, the alphabet, colors, and shapes.

This age group can usually start using metal, blunt scissors. Your child should be encouraged to make creative decisions, such as what colors to use or what shapes to cut. It is also a good time for her to learn to share and take turns with her craft supplies.

Getting Ready for School Book

Kids will usually love the idea of practicing to get ready for school. This book will make them feel special and offer them a way to keep all of their "work" together.

Three-ring binder
Loose-leaf paper with binder holes
Crayons, colored pencils, or markers
Stickers

1. Encourage your child to decorate the binder. She can use stickers, markers, or anything else she likes to personalize it.
2. Fill the binder with paper. If you like, you can also buy a plastic pencil case/pouch that can be stored in the binder so all of the supplies stay together.
3. Have her take the book with her wherever she goes, because you never know when the urge to write or color will hit! She can draw pictures of places she has been or things she has seen, or she can draw abstract designs. You may want to date each page and also write down her description of each picture.
4. You can have the child work on skills to help her get ready for school, such as writing her name or working with specific colors. You can also help her recognize shapes, numbers, and letters.

Sock Puppet

Kids will love creating their own sock characters using a variety of craft supplies, and this is a great way to use up any orphaned socks.

Socks
Craft glue
Miscellaneous craft supplies (yarn, buttons, pom-poms, felt, feathers, etc.)
Scissors
Markers

1. Give the child a sock and a variety of miscellaneous craft supplies. You may have to help him cut some of the supplies, because the safety scissors may not be strong enough. You can also have a variety of items cut ahead of time.

ELSEWHERE ON THE WEB

▶ If you are curious about what stage your child is going through, check out this Development Tracker at http://parenting.ivillage.com/0,,devtrkr_9r7d,00.html. Choose the appropriate age, and this guide shows you important milestones and skills you can expect. There is information that helps you follow your child's development from the toddler years through twelfth grade. You'll find a range of skills for each age, from academic abilities to social development.

2. Let him glue the craft supplies onto the sock to create his own puppet.
3. He can draw facial and other features using markers. He can also use fabric paint, but keep in mind that it takes a long time to dry.

Lacing Cards

This project takes some adult preparation, but, once completed, the kids will enjoy playing with it for hours.

Coloring-book page	Scissors
Crayons	Hole puncher
Thin cardboard	Yarn
Glue	Masking tape

1. Have your child find a picture in a coloring book, rip it out, and have her color it.
2. Glue the picture onto the blank side of the cardboard, then cut around the picture to make a simple shape.
3. Use the hole puncher to make holes around the outside edge of the picture, about 1" apart and about ½" from the edge.
4. Cut a piece of yarn about 26" long, although this may have to be adjusted depending on how big your design is.
5. Wrap one end of the yarn with a little bit of masking tape so it is easier for your child to thread through the holes. Tie the other end of the yarn through one of the holes you punched. Show her how to "sew" the card.

Alphabet Soup

Everyone loves alphabet soup! Though this craft isn't edible, it is a fun way for a child to practice letter recognition.

Poster board
Construction paper
Scissors
Alphabet-shaped cereal or noodles
Glue

1. Cut a large circle out of the construction paper. This will be your bowl. Then cut another circle shape out of a lighter-colored piece of construction paper, about ½" smaller than your first circle. Next, cut a spoon shape using a contrasting piece of construction paper. (You can trace a real spoon.)
2. Have your child glue the smaller circle on top of the poster-board circle. The smaller circle (the poster-board circle) will be the "soup broth" in the bowl.
3. Next, have him glue the spoon near the edge of the bowl.
4. Now comes the fun part! He gets to make his alphabet soup by gluing alphabet cereal or noodles onto the broth. The easiest way is to give him a small bowl of glue and a cotton swab, and have him dot the glue onto the paper and then stick the cereal or noodles to it.
5. Challenge him to write his name and other words using the cereal or noodles.

Crafts for Elementary School Kids

Crafts are a great way to entertain kids when they are bored, as well as a great way to get them away from the television! This age group has usually mastered the use of scissors enough to be

ELSEWHERE ON THE WEB

▶ For a large selection of crafts and activities for elementary-school kids, visit the Enchanted Learning Web site (www.enchantedlearning.com). This is a great educational site kids will enjoy exploring with you. Kids can learn more about topics that interest them, and also make unique, related crafts. There is also a large collection of printable worksheets, coloring-book pages, and even printable books.

Front of completed piggy bank

trusted using regular scissors. While they do enjoy the process of crafting, they also look forward to the finished project and take pride in the work they do.

Piggy Bank

This is a fun way to recycle a nut container or potato-chip cylinder. It is also a good way to motivate kids to save money.

Any cylinder with	Paint
a resealable lid	Felt
Chenille stems	Large wiggle eyes
Glue	Craft knife (for adult use only!)
Paintbrush	Scissors

1. Before your child starts working on the project, use the craft knife and cut a slit in the lid of the container that is big enough for large coins to slip through.
2. Have your child paint the container and lid. For a more traditional pig, he can paint it pink or beige, but he can certainly paint it any color or add any designs he likes. Put it aside to dry.
3. Cut a 2" oval from the felt for the nose, and two small circles of a contrasting color for the nostrils. Cut out two small triangles for the ears, and cut a few inches off of the end of the chenille stem and wrap that piece around a pen or pencil to make it look like a spiral for the tail.
4. Once the container is dry, replace the lid. Glue the two ears across from each other on the side of the lid. Center the nose between the two ears and glue it toward the center of the container. Glue the eyes just above the nose, and glue on the nostrils. Glue the tail onto the container opposite the nose.

Decorated Pencils

Have your child make a handful of these fun pencils to use at school or to give as gifts.

Pencils
Chenille stems
Pom-poms
Miscellaneous craft supplies (wiggle eyes, feathers,
    felt scraps, etc.)
Glue

1. Have your child wrap one end of the chenille stem around the eraser end of a pencil so it spirals around the pencil and stays in place.
2. Leave 1" or 2" of the other end of the chenille stem straight above the top of the eraser.
3. Have her place a dab of glue on a pom-pom and poke it onto the end of the chenille stem.
4. She can add wiggle eyes, a mouth, nose, arms, or other features using a variety of miscellaneous craft supplies.

Check-Box Camera

This is another fun project that can be played with long after the crafting is done.

Empty check box	Construction paper
Tape	Markers
White paper	Crayons or colored pencils
Scissors	

WHAT'S HOT

▶ Personalized pens and pencils can be a great fashion accessory for school. Kids' pens and pencils can match their favorite outfit or show their school spirit. Your kids can express themselves by embellishing their writing tools using a variety of craft supplies. You can find dozens of ideas, along with ideas to make fun pencil holders, on this page: http://about.com/familycrafts/penspencils.

1. Open the check box. Lay the bottom half of the box onto a white piece of paper and trace around it. Cut out the rectangle so it is about ½" smaller than the box on all sides. Using this piece as a template, cut out at least twelve pieces of paper this size, and set aside.

2. Have your child use tape to cover the outside of both the lid and the bottom of the check box with construction paper. Make sure all of the edges are taped down. Encourage him to use markers to draw details on the camera, such as the lens, viewfinder, and flash. If he prefers, he can use miscellaneous craft supplies to add these features.

3. Now for the fun part: All of those white rectangles you cut out earlier are going to be the pictures he takes! They can go inside the camera, and when he takes a pretend picture, he can open the camera back and take out a picture.

4. Your child can draw the pictures as he takes them, or ahead of time. Another option would be to cut pictures of people, places, and things out of magazines and glue them to the papers.

Crafts for Tweens

By the time a kid is what is commonly called a "tween" (approximately ages eleven to fourteen), she can pretty much do an entire craft project by herself. While she has mastered many of the skills needed to complete even the most detailed crafts, she enjoys exploring and experimenting with different craft techniques.

This is sometimes a tough age, so crafting is a good tool to use to try to put a smile on her face and take her mind off of stress. Plus, it is a good way to get her away from the television, the computer, and video games.

TOOLS YOU NEED

▶ I ran across this Web site and think it is a valuable tool for parents of both tweens and teens: Tweens and Teens News at www.tweensand teensnews.com. The site calls itself a parenting guide for parents with kids ages ten and over. The teenage years can be tough on both kids and parents, and this online magazine has some wonderful resources, useful advice, and fun articles.

Locker Message Board

This magnetic notepad holder is perfect for a locker, but will also work on the refrigerator or anywhere else the magnets will stick.

Craft foam	Ribbon
Pen or pencil	Magnets (you will need five pieces,
Glue	about 1" square)
Scissors	Hole puncher

1. Cut a piece of craft foam approximate 5" × 7".
2. Using the scissors, cut a slit about 4" long, starting about ½" from one 7" side and stopping about ½" from the other 7" side. This slit should be about ½" from one of the 5" edges.
3. Cut another piece of craft foam approximately 7" × 9". Glue on the magnets, one in each corner and one in the center, onto what will be the back of the message board.
4. Run a thin bead of glue around the edge of the 5" × 7" piece of foam with the slit (the slit is nearest to the top edge). Stick it, centered, onto the large craft-foam piece on the side without the magnets.
5. Punch a hole near one of the top corners of the larger craft-foam sheet.
6. Cut a piece of ribbon about 18" long. Tie one end of the ribbon to the pen or pencil and the other end to the hole you punched in the craft foam.
7. Once the glue is dry, slip the piece of cardboard from the back of a small tablet of paper into the slot in the craft foam and hang up your locker message board.

CD Holder

Make fancy CD holders for all of your tunes.

Craft foam	¼" ribbon
Hook and loop tape	Craft-foam letters
Scissors	Hole puncher
Glue	

1. Cut the craft foam so it is approximately 6½" × 12", then fold the piece in half so it is 6½" × 6".
2. You will use a hole puncher and make holes about ½" from the side through both thicknesses of craft foam. (You may have to punch one hole and then line up the craft foam to punch the other holes evenly.) Start on one side near the folded edge and work up that side, with your punches about 1" apart. Then do the same thing on the other side, directly across from the holes on the first side.
3. Cut two pieces of ribbon, at least 24" long. Starting at the top of the CD holder (the unpunched edge that is open), thread one end of the ribbon through the first set of holes so there is at least 6" left hanging. Thread the same end of the ribbon through the next set of holes, starting from the same side, so you almost get a spiral effect going down the side of the CD case. When you get to the last hole, work your way back up in the same fashion. Tie the ribbon-ends together when you get back to the top hole and trim them so they are even. The sides can actually be laced up in whatever way you are comfortable with. Lace the second side like you did the first.
4. Cut a small piece of both the hook and loop tape, about ½" squared. Glue the back side of each piece just inside the top edge of the CD case so it can be closed. Let the glue dry.

5. Use the craft-foam letters, or anything else you like, to personalize your CD case.

Decorated Journal

These can be used as private journals or taken to school and used as class notebooks.

Small notebook or journal (the black and white composition journals available at most stores work great)
2 pieces of fabric in coordinating colors
2 pieces of cardboard (at least as big as the notebook cover)
Craft glue
Pen or pencil
Scissors

1. The fabric should be laid on the work surface, right-side-down.
2. Center the notebook on top of the fabric and lightly trace around it.
3. Cut out the fabric so it is about 2" larger than the drawn line.
4. Again, lay the fabric flat on the work surface, right-side-down, and center the opened notebook on the fabric.
5. Dab glue on the inside of the notebook cover and gently pull the overlapped fabric onto the glue. Do this all of the way around your notebook until the outside is completely covered with fabric. You may have to trim the fabric down and trim around the binding to make the fabric lay flat.
6. Cut two pieces of cardboard about ½" smaller than the cover of the notebook.
7. Cut two pieces of the second fabric about 2" larger than your pieces of cardboard and glue to the cardboard, wrapping the edges around the edges like you did with the notebook.

ELSEWHERE ON THE WEB

▶ There is a Web site I ran across that I think parents should urge their tweens and teens to visit. It's called It's My Life, and can be found at http://pbskids.org/itsmylife/index.html. This site, hosted by PBS, shares stories and gives advice to this age group, as well as offering games, activities, fun quizzes, polls, and more. Their main goal is to show tweens that whatever issues they are dealing with, other tweens and teens have gone through the same thing.

8. Glue the covered cardboard on the inside of the notebook covers so all of the glued sides are sandwiched together and hidden. Let the glue dry.
9. The cover can now be personalized and embellished any way you want.

Crafts for Teens

Teenagers may think they are grown-up, but most like nothing better than sitting down and crafting, as it brings back memories from when they were young. By the time they are teens, many kids have a favorite craft, such as scrapbooking, knitting, or woodworking. Still, some of the following simple crafts might spark their interest.

Custom Frames

These decorated frames not only look fabulous on a dresser, they make a great gift for a special friend.

Cheap picture frame
Spray paint
Embellishing items (buttons, plastic gems, beads, dimensional paint, stickers, etc.)
Glue
Photographs

1. Take the back off of the frame and remove the glass. Set them aside.
2. Set the frame on a covered surface, preferably outdoors, and spray paint it using several thin coats.
3. Once the paint is dry, the frame can be embellished. First, find the photo or photos to go into the frame so the embellish-

ments can be planned accordingly. Perhaps "Best Friends" can be written with dimensional paint, or the entire frame can be spotted with colorful buttons.

Tin-Can Candle Holder

These unique candle holders are fun to create, make cool decorations, and are welcomed gifts.

Tin can
Paper
Duct tape
Nail
Hammer

1. Wash your can well and remove the label. Measure your can so you know how big you need to draw your design.
2. Fill your tin can with water, leaving about 1" of room from the top edge. Put it in the freezer and leave until the water is frozen solid.
3. While your can of water is freezing, you can plan your design. Using the measurements you took, you can draw a design on a piece of paper using dots. This will give you a guideline to follow once you start working on your can.
4. Take the can out of the freezer once frozen, and tape your design around it. Use the hammer and nail to tap holes into the can and ice, following the dots on your pattern.
5. When your design is complete, remove your pattern and let the ice melt.
6. Once your can is dry, you can place a candle inside and light it.

ASK YOUR GUIDE

My child does not like to craft. What can i do?

▶ This is not something that should be forced. Crafting is supposed to be enjoyable, and a great way to have some quality time together. if even one of you is miserable doing it, then the purpose is lost. Don't be discouraged, though, there are many things a parent can do to nurture a child's creativity. Check out the list at www .artistshelpingchildren.org/ articlemurphy.html for ideas on how to get their creative juices flowing.

Get Linked

While I give the age suggestions for these crafts, the best judge as to whether or not your child can handle these crafts is you. Your goal is to have your child enjoy himself without getting frustrated. You will find many more projects in this book that are suitable for various ages, and many can be modified to suit any age. You can also check out these resources on my About.com site.

PICTURES OF CHAPTER 4 CRAFTS

Visit this link to see colored photos of all of the craft projects shared in this chapter. You can also share photos or crafts you've completed.

http://about.com/familycrafts/chapter4

CRAFT PROJECTS BY AGE

Here you will find hundreds of free craft projects sorted by age.

http://about.com/familycrafts/projectsbyage

Chapter 5

Crafts from Trash

Why Turn Trash into Treasures?

Many of us know we should recycle rather than tossing everything into the garbage. And what better way to recycle than to use the items you might normally throw away as craft supplies? Recycling can also save you money. Instead of stocking your craft cupboard full of store-bought supplies, consider filling it with recyclables. You will be amazed at what you can create using items such as CDs, magazines, egg cartons, plastic grocery bags, and more.

There are just a few concerns that should be addressed when it comes to working with recycled items. These concerns should not deter you from using trash in your crafts, because they can usually be taken care of quite easily.

First of all, there is some controversy about using certain recyclable items in crafting, especially with children. Some people worry that there might be bacteria or other contaminants left on the items from their original contents. While these concerns are valid, they can be easily remedied. Before you reuse these items in

About.

Do film containers have toxic residue or chemicals?

▶ Contrary to what you may have heard, the answer is no. This comes directly from the people at Kodak: "The chemicals in a roll of film are embedded in the gelatin emulsion layers and do not rub off the plastic film base. The gelatin used in film is more highly refined than that used in common gelatin-based desserts." The biggest concern is the choking hazard they present to younger children. You can read Kodak's entire message here: http://about.com/familycrafts/film containersafety.

crafts, you should make sure they are thoroughly washed in hot, soapy water and then left to air dry. This goes for any item you are recycling, except, of course, paper-based products.

Another concern is the condition of some recycled items. For example, once opened, tin cans tend to have sharp edges that need to be covered or smoothed out. You should make sure all items being used for crafting are free of sharp edges and dangerous points. You also want to make sure there are no small parts that can pose a choking hazard to younger children.

For the most part, using commonsense will take care of most of these issues, but sometimes you have to get creative to get the results you are looking for. No matter what you are using to craft or what end result you are looking for, remember, a little imagination and ingenuity goes a long way!

Bottle Caps and Jar Lids

You can create everything from decorative frames to refrigerator magnets using bottle caps, jar lids, and frozen-juice can covers. One of the nice things about working with these trash items is that they are small, so you don't need a large space to store a large collection of them.

Bottle-Cap Frame

Embellish a plain, inexpensive acrylic frame with a variety of decorated bottle caps.

Metal bottle caps
Rubber mallet
Acrylic paint
Acrylic spray sealer
Miscellaneous pictures or letters

Double-sided tape or adhesive
Strong glue (E6000 or Gorilla Glue)
Liquid laminate (optional)
Paintbrush
Scissors

1. Place your bottle caps, top-side-up, on a hard surface and gently pound on them to flair out the edges.
2. To decorate your bottle caps, think about what picture you will be putting in the frame. If it is a picture of you and a friend, consider using seven bottle caps to spell out the word "FRIENDS" (one letter per cap). If it's a picture of a pet, you can spell out its name, or use small pictures of items related to your pet, such as dog bones, a mouse, etc.
3. You can start out by painting your bottle caps. Once the paint is dry, you can seal the paint using the acrylic spray sealer. This is a good idea if your finished project may be in contact with any moisture, plus it can add a nice shine to your painted surface.
4. While the paint/acrylic sealer is drying, find the letters or pictures you will use to embellish your bottle caps. Your best options are to use magazine pictures or stickers. You can use photos or pictures printed from a computer, but you should get copies made of these, because your printer ink may run. Cut your pictures down so they are a small circle that can fit into the bottle cap. Use double-sided tape or adhesive to secure these inside the cap. If desired, seal the pictures inside the bottle caps using liquid laminate (follow directions on the bottle).
5. Once your bottle caps are dry, you can glue them onto your frame however you like.

WHAT'S HOT

▶ Using bottle caps is a popular trend in scrapbooking and other paper crafts. Of course, the bottle caps used in scrapbooking are usually purchased, not recycled, because if they come in contact with photos they should be of archival quality. But, if you are making greeting cards or other similar paper products, you can use recycled bottle caps rather than paying the high price for specialized ones.

Jar-Lid Clickers

You can make these tiny noise makers using a pair of jar lids (baby-food jar lids work well) and a few other supplies.

2 metal jar lids of the same size	¼" elastic
	Glue
Hammer	Nail
Miscellaneous embellishing supplies (see below)	Paintbrush
	Scissors

1. Place the jar lids on a firm surface and use the hammer and nail to punch a hole in the center of each lid. Cut two pieces of elastic, about 5" long. Push both ends of the piece of elastic through the holes so you have a loop on the top side of the lid that your finger can slide into. Tie the ends of the elastic together so they don't slide back out of the hole. Secure the knot in place with a generous dab of glue.
2. You can now decorate the top of your clickers with miscellaneous items such as felt, glitter, paint, sequins, or just about any other small craft item you can find.
3. Once any glue or paint is dry, you can slip one clicker onto the tip of your index finger, slip the other clicker onto the tip of your thumb, and lightly tap the clickers together to make wonderful music!

Lid Magnets

Make these magnets for your own refrigerator, a school locker, or to give as gifts to your friends, coworkers, and family.

TOOLS YOU NEED

▶ When it comes to making holes in craft objects, sanding down rough edges, and other smaller jobs, you may want to consider getting a rotary tool. They are similar to a drill, spinning at a high rate of speed. However, rotary tools are smaller and come with a large selection of attachments that can help you accomplish many tasks, including drilling, sanding, grinding, and engraving.

Frozen-juice can lids, bottle caps, plastic-bottle lids, etc.
Embellishment items
Craft glue and/or double-sided tape or adhesive
Strong glue (E6000 or Gorilla Glue)
Magnets
Paintbrush
Scissors

1. You can start with any lid as the base; my favorites are juice-can lids because there is a larger, smoother surface to work with. Use the strong glue to attach the magnet to what would have been the top of the bottle cap or lid. Let the glue dry.

2. You can make a magnet with photos of your favorite people or pets. Simply cut the photo to size and glue it onto the inside of the bottle cap or lid. You can hide the background a little by tracing around the picture with dimensional paint (sometimes referred to as squeezable fabric paint). This adds a nice raised edge around your photo. You can use different colors of dimensional paint and even blend them using the tip of a toothpick. You can also make magnet critters by covering the bottle cap or lid with felt or fake fur. Add a felt mouth, wiggle eyes, and any other features you desire.

CDs

Have you ever gotten unsolicited CDs in the mail? Many Internet Service Providers send them often. Next time you are tempted to throw away a CD from the mail or an outdated collection, try some of these projects.

ELSEWHERE ON THE WEB

▶ Magnets are really fascinating. Not only can you make a variety of crafts with them, you can learn a lot by using them. It you want to find more magnet activities and crafts, check out Magnet Man's Web site at www.cool magnetman.com. Explore his Cool Experiments with Magnets and you will not only find fun activities, you will learn more than you ever wanted to know about magnets!

CD Sun Catcher

This seems to be an obvious choice, since most CDs are metallic and catch/reflect the light well. These make great gifts or party decorations, and can be used indoors or out.

2 to 6 unwanted CDs	Craft glue
Work gloves	Nail
Matches or lighter	Craft wire
Beads	Wire cutters

▶ Crafting with wire has come a long way! Wire is not only available in different sizes, it is also available in just about any color you can think of. The tricky part about buying wire comes with understanding the size-numbering system. One might think the higher the number the thicker the wire, but it is actually the opposite. For example, a seed bead (size 11/0) can usually be strung on 28-gauge wire, but 18 gauge would be too thick.

1. Start out by gluing two CDs together on the label side, so that the blank, shiny sides are facing out. You can use only two CDs for a single-tiered sun catcher; use four CDs for a two-tiered sun catcher, six for a three-tiered sun catcher, and so on.

2. Put a work glove on one hand and hold the head of the nail with that hand. Use the matches or lighter (adults should complete this step for any kids doing this project) and heat the point of the nail. Carefully push the hot tip of the nail through the pair of CDs, about ½" from the outer edge. This will create a hole you can string wire through to hang up your sun catcher. You may have to heat the nail tip more than once to make a clean hole through both CDs. Test the hole with the wire to make sure it is big enough for the wire to fit through. Adjust as needed. You now need to make a second hole, directly across from the first hole, again about ½" from the outer edge. Repeat this same step for all of your glued CD pairs.

3. The gauge of the wire you will use will depend on what kind of beads you use. A gauge ranging 24 to 26 works best for smaller beads. Cut a 5" to 7" piece of wire for each hole you made in the CDs. Starting with what will be your top CD, thread about 1" of one end of a piece of wire through one of the holes. Twist

the end around the wire right next to the edge of the CD, so the wire is firmly attached to the CD. String some beads onto the other end of the wire, pushing them down so they rest near the edge of the CD. When you have about 3" of wire left, twist the end down and wrap it around the wire just above the beads to make a loop for hanging.

4. Take a second piece of wire and string it through the second hole in your CD pair, then twist to secure as you did with the first wire. Once again, string beads onto the wire. This time you will only need to leave about 1" at the end of the wire free of beads. If you are making your sun catcher with only one tier, simply fold up the end of this wire so that the beads stay in place. If you are making a sun catcher with two or more tiers, thread the end of this wire through one of the holes you made in another set of CDs. Attach all of your CD pairs together in this manner, leaving a dangling wire full of beads on your last CD.

5. If desired, you can decorate your sun catcher by drawing designs using dimensional paint or glitter, or by gluing on flat gems.

CD Bowls

Believe it or not, you can create little bowls out of CDs. Make sure you do this craft in a well-ventilated area. Any children working on this project should be closely supervised. I would suggest having the adult deal with the heating of the CD and let any children be involved with decorating the cooled CD bowls.

Unwanted CD	Aluminum foil
Cookie sheet	Craft foam or felt
Acrylic paint	Acrylic spray sealer
Paintbrush	Scissors

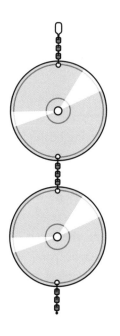

▶ If you are in need of large quantities of recycled items, consider contacting businesses in your area. Call your doctor or dentist office and ask them what they do with their outdated magazines and newspapers; these can be used for collages, paper mache, and other projects. Contact a photographer or store that develops film and see if they can donate some film containers. Many businesses will be happy to help—and get rid of unwanted items!

1. Heat the oven to 325 degrees. Cover a cookie sheet with foil. Use more foil to make a small ball (this will serve as the mold for your bowl). This can be just about any size or shape you like, depending on the shape you want your finished bowl to be. The main thing you should keep in mind is that when the CD starts to soften and melt, the edges will gently fold over, and you do not want the edges to touch the cookie-sheet surface. A good size to start with is a foil ball 2" to 3" × 2" to 3". This should give you a nice-sized bowl with fluted edges.

2. When you get the foil ball to the desired shape and size, place it on the foil-lined cookie sheet. Then, place a CD on top of the ball so the side with the writing or label is facing up. Carefully slide the cookie sheet in the oven and watch it closely. It may take as long as 10 minutes for the CD to soften and fold down around the foil ball. Remove the cookie sheet from the oven when the bowl is shaped the way you want it. You can use an oven mitt to further shape the warm CD if you like. Allow the CD to cool and harden.

3. Once cool, the bowl can be removed from the foil ball and used or embellished as desired. You can paint the outside to cover the label and then spray it with clear acrylic sealer. You can use a circle cut from craft foam or felt to cover the hole in the bottom of the bowl by gluing it to the inside or outside of the bowl. You can also embellish the bowl with plastic gems, beads, etc. Experiment and have fun with lots of different depths, widths, and shapes.

Egg Cartons

Egg cartons are, perhaps, one of the more commonly reused trash items. There are many crafts to make with these, but the following are a few of my favorites.

Jewelry or Desk Organizer

By design, egg cartons are an obvious choice for organizing and storing small objects. However, an undecorated egg carton would look out of place sitting on a desk or dresser. Using simple craft supplies, you can decorate an egg carton to match your decor.

Clean, dry egg carton	Acrylic paint
Scrap fabric	Glue
Decoupage medium	Clear acrylic spray
Paintbrush	Small foam brush
Scissors	

1. Start out by painting the entire egg carton. While it is drying, prepare your fabric by cutting it to fit. Fit what, you may ask? Well, that depends on your fabric and what you like. I would first consider covering the entire top of the egg carton by gluing on a rectangle of fabric. If your fabric has a cute motif, consider cutting out individual designs and gluing them onto the egg carton separately.

2. Once all of the glue and paint is dry, apply thin coats of the decoupage medium with the foam brush to seal the fabric to the box. This should only take a few thin coats (make sure each coat is totally dry before adding another coat). Once you are happy with the number of coats you have applied, and after the decoupage medium is dry, spray the entire egg carton with the clear acrylic spray. Again, you may need to apply several

What is clear acrylic spray and what is it used for?

▶ This is a spray sealer used to add a permanent finish to completed projects to make them more resistant to the elements, and is especially good for adding a tough, clear finish to almost anything, including some photos, maps, carbon copies, and printed pages. I have used them to help make home-printed business cards water resistant! You can usually find it in a matte or gloss finish.

thin coats until you get the finish and shine that you are happy with.

3. Once your egg-carton organizer is dry, proudly use and display it. As a jewelry box, it can sort and hold rings, earrings, cufflinks, etc. As a desk organizer, you can use it to hold small items like paper clips, rubber bands, push pins, etc.

Egg-Carton Bouquet

Create a variety of beautiful flowers using cups cut from egg cartons and a few other supplies.

Clean, dry egg carton	Acrylic paint
Craft sticks (popsicle sticks)	Chenille stems
Green felt or craft foam	Craft glue
Paintbrush	Scissors

1. Cut the egg carton into individual cups. Cut around the top of each cup to shape the edges like a flower. You can cut pointy petals to look like a tulip, rounded petal shapes, or a combination of both. Once all of your flowers' petals are cut, paint them as desired. At this time, also paint both sides of your craft sticks green; paint as many sticks as you have flowers.

2. Once the paint is dry, put a dab of glue on the back/bottom side of the egg-carton cup and stick the flower to one of the flat sides of a craft stick. The flower should be all of the way to one end of the craft stick, so the stick acts as a stem. You can cut leaf shapes out of green felt or craft foam and glue them onto the stems.

3. Embellish the flowers further by cutting 3" to 4" pieces from the chenille stems to make a stamen. Fold the piece of chenille

stem in half, dab the fold generously with glue, and press it into the center of your egg-cup flower.

4. Your flowers are now done and ready to give or display. An easy way to display them is to put some floral foam in a small clay pot and press the ends of the flowers into the foam.

Egg-Carton Disguise

Everyone will have a ball not only creating these fun disguises, but also wearing them. They are easy to make and can be as simple or as fancy as you choose.

Egg carton	Acrylic paint
Construction paper	¼" elastic
Craft glue	Masking tape
Paintbrush	Scissors
Miscellaneous embellishment items (see below)	

1. You can make wearable noses, eyes, and even ears using egg-carton cups. They can resemble animals, mythical creatures, or they can just be goofy. To make any of these, start out by cutting the egg carton into individual cups.

2. To make a nose, you need one egg-carton cup, a piece of elastic long enough to fit around your head, paint, and any items you want to use to embellish your nose. Start out by painting the outside of your egg-carton cup whatever color you want and letting it dry. Then add any embellishments, such as whiskers, a pom-pom point, nose ring, freckles, and so on. Once you have your nose decorated, use the point of the scissors and poke two holes, directly across from each other, toward the open end on the sides of the egg-carton cup. String one end of the elastic into each hole, from the painted side in. Tie

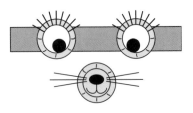

a knot in the end of each end to secure. Try your nose on to make sure the elastic fits, then tape the ends to make sure they stay in place.

3. To make eyes to go along with your nose, start out by making a paper headband about 1" thick that fits around your forehead. Now decorate your disguise eyes (the outside of two egg-carton cups) as desired. Start by painting them, and then embellish to your heart's content. Once the paint and/or glue on your disguise eyes are dry, glue the eyes onto the headband.

4. If you want to wear funky ears, you should make them and then attach them to the sides of the headband you made your eyes on. Starting at the top edge, cut an egg-carton cup in half so you have two halves that look like mirror images of each other. This time, instead of decorating the outside of the egg-carton cup, the inside will be what is facing out. Once you get your ears decorated as desired, glue them onto the headband so they will sit on the sides of your head.

Film Containers

These little black containers are great craft items, but with digital and disposable cameras growing in popularity, these containers are getting harder to find. If you can't get your hands on empty film containers, you can substitute empty pill bottles.

Emergency-Kit Necklace

Although this idea may sound silly, you will be happy you have one of these little kits if you need it. There are many variations, and I bet you can think of even more. Let this list be your guide, and add items that work best for your needs.

Empty film container   Nail
Matches or a lighter   ¼" ribbon
Craft glue   Embellishment items
Scissors   (read below)
Kit items (see below)

1. Put a work glove on one hand and hold the head of the nail with this hand. Use the matches or a lighter (adults should complete this step for any kids doing this project) and heat the pointed end of the nail. Carefully push the hot tip of the nail through the lid of the film container or pill bottle. You will want it just a little off center. Reheat the nail and poke another hole, just off center, across from the other hole. Make sure both holes are big enough that the ends of a piece of your ribbon can be poked through them.

2. Cut a piece of ribbon about 30" long. Thread each end of the ribbon through each hole you made in the lid. Place the ribbon around your neck to make sure it hangs where you want it and tie the ends together to secure. Place a dab of glue on the knot and glue it to the inside of the lid just to make sure the ribbon doesn't slip off. Put the lid back on your container and your necklace is almost ready to wear!

3. Before you wear your necklace, you may want to decorate it. You can cover the container with paper or paint it with acrylic paint or even nail polish. You can dress up your necklace with stickers, glitter, sequins, or gemstones.

4. Now you can fill your emergency kit. Here are some suggestions to get you started:

ELSEWHERE ON THE WEB

▶ To learn more about how to creatively recycle and find some great craft projects, drop by The Imagination Factory at www.kid-at-art.com. This is an award-winning arts and crafts site for kids, parents, and teachers. You can start out by reading the current article, then browse through projects listed either by trash item used or by the project type. They even have a special section listing projects that help to fulfill Scout badge requirements.

▶ Recycling-related arts and crafts have been popular for quite a while, but now it seems to be going by a different name: altered art. Serious artists have brought new respect to recycling with their creations made from CDs, cigar boxes, hardbound books, candy tins, and much more. I have a section on my Web site that features a variety of altered-art projects and resources that can be found here: http://about.com/familycrafts/alteredart.

- **First-Aid kit:** Band-Aids, alcohol wipe, cotton ball, safety pin, aspirin
- **Sewing kit:** Needle, bobbin full of thread, safety pin, thimble, button
- **Survival kit:** Safety pin, small wrapped candy, money, paper with phone numbers
- **Clean-hands kit:** Fill with hand sanitizing lotion
- **Pony kit:** Ponytail holders, bobby pins, barrettes

Finger Puppets

This is a great project that does double duty. First, it is a fun craft project that encourages everyone to design his own finger-puppet characters. It is also a great activity to help pass the time. After the puppets are made, take time to put on a special puppet show.

Empty film container	Felt or craft foam
Wiggle eyes	Pom-poms
Chenille stems	Craft glue
Scissors	

Simply turn the empty container over, embellish, and slip it on your finger. You can create a wide variety of finger-puppet characters using a variety of supplies. Cut ears, arms, and other body parts out of felt or craft foam and glue them in place. You can use small pom-poms for noses, and don't forget the wiggle eyes! Use your imagination and entertain everyone!

Tooth Saver

This is a great project to make with or for kids who are getting ready to start losing their teeth.

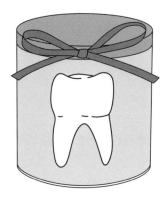

Empty film container
¼"-thick ribbon
Thin-tipped marker
Craft glue

White contact paper
White craft foam
Hole punch
Scissors

1. Draw about six small, molar-shaped patterns on the white contact paper—you will want these no more than 1" high. Cut them out, peel off the back, and stick them randomly onto the film container to decorate it.

2. Next, draw a larger molar shape on the white craft foam—you will want this one about 2" high. Cut it out and punch a hole toward the top of it. Using the thin-tipped marker, write "For the Tooth Fairy" or something similar on this tooth-shaped gift tag.

3. Cut a piece of ribbon about 20" long. Tie it around the side edge of the lid of the container and secure it with some glue. Slip the tooth-shaped gift tag onto one of the ends of the ribbon, and then tie the ribbon in a bow. Trim the ends if they are too long, and place a dab of glue on the knot so it stays tied. Set the tooth saver aside to dry.

4. Your child can take this with her so she has a place to store a tooth if she loses one. It is also handy for putting a lost tooth under the pillow, and the tooth fairy can put any treats inside it when she collects the tooth. If you like, you can also turn this into a handy necklace by following the directions provided earlier for making film-container emergency-kit necklaces.

Get Linked

Now, I hope you have gained a new respect for your garbage and its creative possibilities. Start saving those trash items, and the next time you are bored, pull them out and see what you can create. You just might surprise yourself! If you would like to learn more about how to creatively recycle a variety of items, check out these resources on my About.com site:

PICTURES OF CHAPTER 5 CRAFTS

Visit this link to see colored photos of all of the craft projects shared in this chapter. You can also share photos or crafts you've completed.
http://about.com/familycrafts/chapter5

TRASH TO TREASURE

Enjoy this collection of ideas for using the things you might normally throw away to create great craft projects, games, and more. The projects are sorted by the trash item used.
http://about.com/familycrafts/trashtreasure

Chapter 6

Home Crafts

For the Bathroom

Sometimes we spend our time making unique crafts, but then have no idea what to do with the finished project. Why not choose a project that you can use around your home when it is done? Besides being used in your home, these ideas would also make great gifts.

Clay-Pot Toothbrush and Soap Holders

This simple craft can be decorated to match your bathroom. For a little more variety, you can decorate these using rub-on decals.

4" terra-cotta pot	5" terra-cotta pot saucer
Flat decorative marbles	Paint
Clear acrylic sealer	Paintbrush

About

1. Paint the clay pot and saucer whatever color you like, then paint on simple shapes, such as squares and circles, using contrasting colors of paint. Let dry.
2. Once the paint is dry, spray them with a few thin layers of clear acrylic sealer. (Spray the sealer in a well-ventilated room with a covered work surface or, better yet, outside.) Let the spray dry.
3. Place the pot and saucer on your bathroom counter and fill them almost full of the flat decorative marbles, one handful at a time (do not pour, as they may break).
4. Place your toothbrushes into the pot by pushing the handle end down into the flat, decorative marbles, and place your soap on top of the marbles. This helps keep the soap from sitting in water and getting soggy.

Cookie-Cutter Soap

Why not make your own soap to put in your new, homemade soap dish? It is easy using this simple recipe and a cookie cutter. For a little variety, you can color your soap using a little bit of food coloring. You can also roll your soap into little balls instead of using cookie cutters.

Mild bar of soap	Warm water
Cookie cutters	Wax paper
Grater	

1. Grate about 1 cup of soap off of the bar. Pour it in a medium-sized mixing bowl.
2. Start with about ¼ cup of the warm water. Pour it into the bowl of grated soap and knead it to mix. Add more water, a little at a time, and continue to knead it until it is the consistency of thick dough.

▶ Rub-on decals are wonderful tools, and they come in a large selection of designs. Once applied, they look and feel like real hand-painted artwork. Applying them requires no tools, water, or glue. You simply hold the decal firmly next to the desired item, carefully rub, and the picture is transferred! You can apply rub-on decals to paper, wood, metal, acrylic, glass, tile, mirror, ceramics, books, walls, photos, furniture, candles, accessories, and more.

3. Set the cookie cutter on a piece of wax paper. Press the soap mixture into the cookie cutter until it is full.

4. If possible, set the cookie cutter on its side, so both sides of your bar of soap can dry. If your bar of soap will not sit on its side, flip it often. Let it dry for about 24 hours.

5. Gently pop your soap out of the cookie cutter. To get the soap out, you may have to carefully bang the cookie-cutter edge on the counter and/or run the sides of the cookie cutter under very warm water.

6. Put it in your soap dish and enjoy!

Glycerin-Soap Surprises

You can make your own little soap bars filled with charms or small toys. These make great gifts for kids (although you should be aware of choking hazards small objects pose to small children) or unique decorations. Parental guidance and supervision is strongly recommended for older kids making this craft. Younger kids enjoy watching this process, but should not be allowed handle the sharp knife and hot glycerin liquid.

> 1 bar clear glycerin
> Small charms, toys, shells, etc.
> Essential oil (optional)
> Molds (see options below)
> Sharp knife

1. Using the knife, cut the glycerin bar into small pieces.

2. Place the glycerin pieces into a microwave-safe bowl (I use a large, Pyrex measuring bowl with pour spout). Microwave on high for 30 seconds and then stir. Continue to microwave for 30-second intervals until it is completely melted. Add the essential oil if desired and mix.

ASK YOUR GUIDE

Will my soap stick to the mold once it hardens?

▶ Yes, it might stick. If you are using a flexible candy or soap mold you can usually twist the mold and the soap will pop out. If you are using something else, you may consider lightly greasing the mold using a very thin coating of shortening, vegetable oil, or even Vaseline. You can also line the mold with plastic wrap. If you would like to learn more about soap making, check this page: http://about.com/familycrafts/soap.

3. Set out your molds on a covered work surface. For a mold, you can use candy or soap molds. If I don't have either of these, I prefer to use doubled (stack one inside of the other), disposable bathroom cups. You can also try ice-cube trays, Styrofoam cups, or pint-size milk cartons with the top cut off.
4. Carefully pour the melted glycerin into the molds so it is about ⅓ full. Let this set for about 5 minutes until it starts to get firm.
5. When the first layer of glycerin is firm enough, carefully set the charm, toys, etc., onto the glycerin. The bottom of your mold will be the top of your soap bar so keep this in mind when positioning your item.
6. Now you can finish filling the mold with the glycerin. You will probably have to reheat it in the microwave after it sits for a while.
7. Let it set for about 30 minutes, or until completely cooled.
8. If you are using a candy or soap mold, you should easily be able to pop out your soap. If using a disposable cup or milk carton, simply tear the paper to reveal the soap.

For the Kitchen

The kitchen is a great place to make use of homemade crafts—and a great place to find craft supplies! The following projects may just make your life in the kitchen a little easier.

Plastic Grocery-Bag Holder

You can sew this simple bag on a machine or by hand—both techniques will be easy. This is a great way to store all of those plastic shopping bags you get almost every time you go to the store.

I kitchen hand towel (approximately 16" × 28")
½"-thick elastic

ELSEWHERE ON THE WEB

▶ My Craft Book is a Web site with a large collection of crafts, including several pages of home and garden crafts. Explore the many projects shared for your kitchen, bathroom, living room, bedroom, and dining room. You can find them here: www.my craftbook.com/Results.asp? categoryID=4.

Ribbon (the color should match the towel)
Scissors
Straight pins
Needle and thread or sewing machine

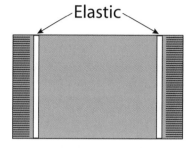

1. Cut two 7"-long pieces of elastic. Cut another piece of elastic about 5" long.
2. Lay the hand towel, design-side-down, on your work surface.
3. Start out by pinning one end of a piece of elastic about ½" from one fringe edge of the towel and flush with the side of the towel. Pin the other end of the elastic directly across from the first end. You have pinned it correctly if you stretch out the elastic and it's a straight line across the edge of the towel.
4. Pin the other piece of elastic in the same fashion on the other end of the towel.
5. To sew, stretch the elastic so it is lying flat, then stitch along the center of the elastic. Sew both sides. Both of the ends of your towel should now gather in as the elastic relaxes.
6. Fold your towel in half, right-sides-together, and sew along the long edge to form a tube, leaving about ½" seam allowance.
7. Fold the ribbon in half to make a loop. Tack this onto one end of the bag, near the sewn theme, to act as a hanger. You can now hang it up and fill it with plastic bags! You can stuff bags into the top of your holder and pull them out through the bottom.

Beaded Recipe Saver

This handy combination recipe holder and space marker can be neatly tucked out of the way when you aren't using it, although it is pretty enough that you may want to find a spot to display it!

20-guage wire	Beads
Pencil	Wire cutters

1. Cut a 16" piece of wire.
2. Start wrapping one end of the wire around the pencil. Wrap 6" of the end to form a tight coil. Slide the coil off of the pencil.
3. String 4" of beads onto the wire.
4. Wrap the straight end of the wire around the pencil as you did with the first end. Once you have a tight coil, carefully slide it off of the pencil.
5. Bend your beaded creation into a "U" shape, and you are done!
6. Set your beaded wire on the counter, and the recipe card can easily be placed in the coils at both ends and be held up for you to read. You can also use the beaded wire to save a spot in your recipe box.

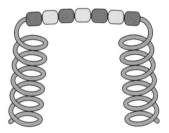

◀ Beaded recipe saver

For the Bedroom

Your bedroom is usually your sanctuary. It's your own personal space in a house shared with others, so why not make some personalized projects to show your style.

Drawer Sachet Pouch

Make one of these simple sachet bags for every drawer, and your nose will get a pleasant surprise every time you open one.

    Tulle or any lightweight fabric
    Ribbon or cording
    Hole puncher
    Potpourri

1. Cut a circle out of your tulle or fabric—tracing around a dinner plate works well.
2. Punch holes around the fabric circle, about 1" in from the edge.
3. Thread a piece of cord or ribbon in and out of the holes. Do not cut the ribbon or cord until you have it threaded into the holes with about 4" to 6" to spare on each end while the fabric is lying flat.
4. Now, simply pull both ends of the cord or ribbon tight to gather the top of the bag together to make a bowl shape. Fill with potpourri. Pull both ends of the cord or ribbon tight to close, and tie.

Doorknob Hanger

Send a message to everyone passing by your room with a customized doorknob hanger.

    Craft foam
    Items to embellish (glitter glue, sequins, gems, etc.)
    Glue
    Scissors

1. Cut out the base for the doorknob hanger. Start out by cutting a 4" × 11" rectangle. Make a 3"-wide circle about 1" from one of the 4" edges. Tracing around a glass is sometimes helpful.
2. Now that you have your base, you can decorate it as you choose. Embellish with glitter glue, sequins, gems, and anything else that you desire. You can also cut letters or shapes out of craft foam (or purchase the precut shapes).
3. You can use the dimensional paint to write messages on your doorknob hanger, such as "Keep Out," "Welcome," "Baby Sleeping," "Please Knock," or "Genius At Work." You can also write one message on one side and the opposite on the other side. When you're done, let it dry. Once it's dry, hang it on your bedroom door!

No-Sew Pillows

Cover pillow forms with fun fabric that matches your room's decor. Experiment with different fabrics to make your own fashion statement.

Pillow form	Fabric
Rubber bands	Ribbon
Scissors	

1. Cut two pieces of fabric, about 3" larger on all four sides than the pillow form.
2. Lay one piece of fabric on your work surface, right side down.
3. Lay the pillow form in the center of the piece of fabric.
4. Lay the second piece of fabric, right side up, onto the pillow form, making sure it's centered.
5. Starting in one corner, grab both points together. Slip a rubber band over the corners, slide it down to the pillow form, and

wrap to tighten. Your corners will now look like two little rabbit ears.

6. Repeat this process with all four corners. Try to make sure the length of the ears are even on all four sides, the fabric along the edges of the pillow is pulled tight, and the raw edge is rolled to the inside so it cannot be seen.

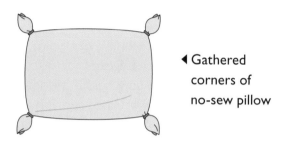

◀ Gathered corners of no-sew pillow

7. To add a finishing touch, tie a piece of ribbon around each rubber band to cover it.

For the Office

Offices are sometimes cold, impersonal rooms. Use these craft projects to add some unique touches to your office, or even just a desktop or locker.

Message Board

You can make a bulletin board for your wall or locker that will hold special messages, notes, and even photographs.

Sheet of ¾"-thick
   Styrofoam
Ribbon

Piece of fabric
Glue
Buttons

Soda-can tabs or
magnet strips
Scissors

Sharp knife
Ruler

1. Use the sharp knife to cut the Styrofoam to the desired size.
2. Cut the fabric so it is 2" to 3" larger than the Styrofoam on all sides.
3. Lay your piece of fabric, right side down, on your work surface.
4. Center the Styrofoam on top of the fabric.
5. Glue the fabric onto one of the long edges of the Styrofoam. I prefer hot glue, simply because of how quickly it dries, but I don't suggest using it with small fingers! Glue your fabric edges down with craft glue and use small pieces of masking tape to hold the edges in place until the glue dries. Let one side dry before gluing the next side. (If you desire, you can also use duct tape to hold the edges of the fabric in place.)
6. Glue the fabric onto the opposite side of the Styrofoam, pulling the fabric tight so it is smooth on the front side.
7. Fold up and glue the two shorter ends like you are wrapping a gift, folding in the sides and then folding up the edge.
8. Once the fabric is glued in place, you can add the ribbon as you please. It is traditionally crossed over itself to make a diagonal grid design. Glue the ends of the ribbon onto the back of your board to hold them in place.
9. Put a dab of glue behind each piece of ribbon where they intersect, and then glue a button on top of that spot for decorative purposes.
10. Glue a few magnet strips or soda-can tabs to the back to use for hanging. To use, messages and photos can simply be tucked between the message board and ribbon to hold them in place without the need for tacks.

TOOLS YOU NEED

▶ Even though they aren't necessary, you can use tacks in the message board featured here. Of course, you wouldn't want to use plain ones! It only takes a few minutes to jazz up plain tacks using items you already have around your house. Put dabs of glue on the head of the tack and glue on buttons, ribbon flowers, colorful beads, or just about any other small object you can find.

Paperweight Rock

This paperweight makes a great gift for someone special. Choose pictures of their favorite hobbies, colors, animals, or people. You can also use photocopied pictures of friends and family members.

Large rock	Magazines
Felt	Glue or decoupage medium
Scissors	Foam glue

1. Select a rock that is large enough to hold papers down and hold a variety of pictures, but that is small enough to handle.
2. Wash the rock and let it dry completely.
3. Cut pictures out of magazines to embellish your rock. You will want to completely cover every inch of the rock except the bottom.
4. Use decoupage techniques to glue the pictures to the rock. Let it dry.
5. Make sure you seal the pictures with a few thin layers of the decoupage medium or watered-down glue.
6. To finish, cut a hunk of felt to fit the bottom of the rock and glue it in place to protect any furniture from being scratched by the rock.

Office-Supply Organizers

Organize everything from pencils to paper clips. You will be able to easily locate any item you're looking for using these erasable labels.

Recyclable containers (shoe boxes, potato-chip cans, frosting containers, etc.)
Wooden beads (4 for each box and 3 for each can)

ASK YOUR GUIDE

What if I want to make a paperweight but I can't find a rock?

▶ Believe it or not, in the event that you cannot find a rock that suits your needs, you can make your own rock! Simply use plaster of Paris to make a rock whatever size and shape you like. You can use a plastic cup or a milk carton, or you can construct a rock-shaped mold using a box, foil, and plastic wrap.

Acrylic paint
Self-adhesive chalkboard or memo-board contact paper
Felt (optional)
Glue
Dimensional paint
Scissors

<WHAT'S HOT>

WHAT'S HOT

▶ Homemade stepping stones are a great way to personalize your garden, walkway, or other area in your yard. They make great gifts and are also nice keepsakes if they are made using children's handprints or footprints. My kids and I had a lot of fun experimenting with our stepping stones. You can find out how to make your own garden stepping stones by reading this article: http://about.com/familycrafts/gardenstones.

1. Make sure any containers you use are clean and free of labels.
2. Paint the outside of the container with acrylic paint. Also paint the wooden beads. Let dry.
3. Line the inside of your container with felt if desired.
4. Glue the wooden beads on the bottom of your container to make feet.
5. Cut a label for each container out of the contact paper. I would suggest a label that will fit one side of the container, but you can use your own judgment.
6. Peel the paper backing off of each label and stick it in place on your container. Make sure there are no air bubbles!
7. Use the dimensional paint to outline the label. This not only adds a decorative finishing touch, it helps to secure the edges of the contact paper to your organizer. Let dry, then use.

For the Garden and Yard

I don't know about you, but I love spending time outside when the weather permits— which sometimes isn't often enough when you live in northern Minnesota! These fun crafts will enhance your outdoor time.

Garden Markers

These fun garden markers not only mark off your garden rows, they also make nice decorations.

Wooden spoons
Acrylic paint
Seed packets or catalogs/magazines
Glue or decoupage medium
Permanent markers
Clear acrylic spray
Paintbrush
Scissors

1. Paint the entire wooden spoon whatever color or colors you desire. Let dry.
2. Cut out pictures of the produce or flowers planted in your garden. The seed packets are great sources, as are catalogs from nurseries. Trim these pictures so they fit in the bowl of the spoon.
3. Glue the pictures onto the bowls of the wooden spoons so that when the handle of the spoon is poked into the ground the picture is not upside down.
4. Let the glue dry and then coat with a few more thin layers of glue or decoupage medium.
5. Use the permanent marker and write the name of the plant running down the handle, starting near the edge of the spoon's bowl.
6. Seal with a few light coats of the clear acrylic sealer. Take your new garden markers outside and poke the handle of the spoon into the ground.

TOOLS YOU NEED

▶ You can find transparent glass paint in any craft store. Like any poster or acrylic paint, it requires nothing more than a paintbrush to apply. If you don't want to invest in transparent glass paint, you can try making your own by mixing glue with a few drops of water and food coloring. This may turn out a tiny bit cloudy, but in some projects that may not matter. Experiment first!

Patio-Light Covers

Start collecting small, plastic water or soda bottles and make your patio or backyard festive with strings of lights using these colorful little covers.

> String of lights
> Small plastic bottles (one for each light on the string)
> Transparent glass paint
> Glue
> Paintbrush
> Scissors and/or craft knife

1. Using the scissors, cut the bottles in half. If you use both halves, you need half as many bottles.
2. Trim down the cut edge by cutting a design you like.
3. Use the tip of the scissors or the craft knife to make a small hole in the half of the bottle that was the bottom. You should be able to slip the light cover over the bulb so that the light covers look like little lamp shades.
4. Paint each light cover using the transparent paint. You can paint the entire light cover or simply paint abstract or other designs.
5. Once all of your light covers are painted and dry, slip them over each light on the string. You may have to use a little bit of glue to secure them so they stay in place. Once any glue is dry, hang up your patio lights and enjoy.

Bagel Bird Feeder

Attract a variety of birds to your backyard with this birdfeeder that will quickly disappear once they discover it.

▸ Most people, kids and adults alike, are fascinated by birds. Birds are mysterious creatures. Have you ever just sat and watched them fly around or listened to them sing their beautiful songs? Have you ever wondered how they can fly, or why they fly south for the winter? You can attract a variety of birds to your yard by making different bird feeders and bird houses like those featured here: http://about.com/family crafts/bird.

½ a stale bagel
1 teaspoon peanut butter
Birdseed
Scissors

String
1 teaspoon shortening
Paper plate

1. Cut a piece of string about 24" long. You can adjust this length depending on where you want to hang it.
2. Put one end of the string through the hole in the bagel and tie both ends together to make a large loop to hang up your bird feeder.
3. Mix together the peanut butter and the shortening. Spread this mixture onto the flat side of the bagel.
4. Pour the birdseed onto the paper plate. Press the peanut butter/shortening side of the bagel into the birdseed.
5. Hang in a tree or anywhere outside and watch the birds enjoy.

For the Playroom

Of course, by nature, playrooms are already fun, but here are a few projects you can add to yours to make it even more fun!

Memory Game

Create your own memory game using lids removed from frozen-juice cans. If your family doesn't drink much juice, you can use little discs cut from cardboard or even index cards.

Juice-can lids
Stickers, die cuts, or magazines/catalogs
Glue
Scissors

ELSEWHERE ON THE WEB

▶ If you would like to try to make a different puzzle, drop by this page at the All Free Craft site: www.allfreecrafts .com/decoupage/decoupage_ puzzle_blocks.shtml. This decoupaged block puzzle is not only a wonderful puzzle, but it would also make a magnificent conversation piece. You can use favorite photos, postcards, and any other pictures that would fit on the blocks.

1. Make sure your juice-can lids are clean and dry. Although you can make as many game pieces as you like, I think twenty is a good starting number. Anything lower than that and the game would be almost too easy! You can always add more pieces later.

2. Gather together your sets of pictures. These can be identical stickers or die-cuts, or pictures cut from magazines. It is easiest if you pick a theme for your game, such as matching colors, matching written numbers to dots, matching lower and upper case letters, matching baby animals to their moms, and so on.

3. Glue or stick your pictures onto one side of each juice-can lid. Let dry. You can also trace around the edges of the pictures using dimensional paint.

4. This game is played like the classic Concentration game that can be played with one or several people. You lay all of the pieces face down. Each player takes turns turning over two pieces at a time. If the pictures match, the player keeps those pieces and gets another turn. If they do not match, the pieces are turned face down again and the next player takes their turn. Continue until all of the game pieces are claimed.

Felt Board

Your child will enjoy helping you make this project, and she'll also enjoy playing with it!

Felt	Large frame
Duct tape	(as large as you desire)
Cardboard to fit frame	Scissors

1. Take the back off of the frame and remove the glass. Save the back and any other cardboard that came with the frame.
2. Cut a piece of cardboard to fit inside the frame. If your frame came with an extra piece of cardboard tucked between the glass and the back, you can use it as long as it is the size of the frame.
3. Cut a piece of felt that is about 2" bigger on all sides than the piece of cardboard.
4. Lay the felt on your work surface and then center your piece of cardboard on top of the felt.
5. Start by taping one edge of the felt to the back of the cardboard, then tape the other edge, pulling it tight to make sure there are no wrinkles on the front of the felt board. Tape the other two edges in the same manner.
6. Place your felt-covered cardboard in the frame so that the felt side faces out. Replace the back of the frame.
7. Your board is now done and, depending on your frame back, you can stand the frame on a dresser or desktop or hang it on the wall.
8. Of course, you can buy a variety of felt shapes at a craft store or school-supply store, but you can also make your own felt-board pieces. You can use stencils or cookie cutters for some shapes. You can also make a pocket for your felt pieces using paper or felt, and if your frame is big enough, you can attach this to the back of the frame using hook and loop tape so they are always together!

Get Linked

If you still want more home-craft ideas, check out these links. Not only will you find great projects for inside your home, you can browse through several projects for your yard, garden, and patio.

PICTURES OF CHAPTER 6 CRAFTS

Visit this link to see colored photos of all of the craft projects shared in this chapter. You can also share photos or crafts you've completed.

http://about.com/familycrafts/chapter6

FOR THE HOME CRAFTS

Directions for making household, yard, and garden decorations and other things you can use or find in or around your house.

http://about.com/familycrafts/homecrafts

Chapter 7

Make It and Wear It

Tie Dye and Other Fabric-Coloring Techniques

There are a whole bunch of products on the market to help you explore the art of fabric dyeing and coloring. You can find everything from fabric dyes and paint to fabric markers and crayons. You can experiment with a variety of techniques such as tie dyeing, spray-painting fabric, fabric coloring, iron-on transfers, and much more.

Which technique and products you use will depend on not only what you are trying to color, but also what kind of effect you are looking for. Every product is different, so make sure you read all labels carefully and follow the directions exactly. Before you invest your time and money into products and techniques that will not serve your needs, read through the different options I've provided.

Before you start experimenting with any of these methods, remember that most of these products were created to stain fabric. That means they will stain clothing, carpets, and sometimes even hands and furniture, so make sure you take any precautions

About®

necessary. Also, you will usually want to prewash any fabric item to be dyed to remove any sizing, which is a substance applied to fabric during the manufacturing process to add stiffness and body. When washing your fabrics after the dyeing or painting process, wash in cold water if they can be washed at all (follow the manufacturer's directions). The first few times they are washed they might bleed, so wash them with like colors or alone.

Experiment with these options and have fun, but more importantly, be safe! When working with younger children, choose a cold-water dye or spend a little more on premixed spray dye. Since many coloring options need to be heat set, adults should make sure kids stay back from irons. Read all of the manufacturer's safety precautions and follow them closely.

Remember simple, old-fashioned tie dyeing? It's easy, and can be done with a plain piece of cloth, a collection of rubber bands or string, and fabric dye. We usually use RIT brand dye, which can be found at most stores, including grocery and discount department stores. This brand is inexpensive, costing only a few dollars per color.

Start out by using the rubber bands or string to tie sections of your fabric. You can fold, twist, or spiral your fabric. Remember, the spots where your fabric is tied will not be dyed. Experiment with different shapes and folds. Secure your rubber bands or string as tight as you can get them.

Prepare your dye as directed by the manufacturer. You should carefully follow all instructions. While preparing the dye and dyeing your item, you should wear rubber gloves to protect your hands from staining. The method you use to mix up your dye and actually dye your fabric will depend on the brand of dye you use. With some dyes you will have to soak your item in soda ash, and with others, like RIT, you simply need to dip it in hot water.

ELSEWHERE ON THE WEB

▶ If you want to research numerous options when it comes to fabric dying, painting, coloring, and transfers, check out Dharma Trading Company's Web site at www.dharmatrading.com. They not only have detailed information and directions for using a large selection of dyes, paints, and so on, they offer these products for sale, along with blank clothing and other textiles. You can spend hours here just reading through all of the wonderful how-to's.

Now you can start dyeing by dipping your fabric into the dye. You can also experiment with spraying or dropping the dye onto the fabric. Use your imagination! It is usually best to start with the lightest color if you are using more than one color. Rinse or wait between colors as directed by the manufacturer.

Make sure to follow all directions carefully when it comes to dyeing and rinsing your items. Some dyes require you to rinse immediately and others require you to let the item sit for at least 24 hours. Some brands may also require you to heat set your fabric, usually by putting it in a clothes dryer.

Batik is another fabric-dying method. With batik, some areas of fabric are covered with wax, glues, or specially made products to keep dyes from penetrating the fabric. Typically, the wax or other product is laid down in a pattern and the paint is applied and allowed to dry. The wax is then removed. The area under the wax keeps its original color, with an occasional line of color giving it a somewhat crackled look.

Traditionally, wax is used as the batik medium. However, if you are working with children, I would suggest experimenting with plain, white school glue instead of wax, since wax must be hot to be applied and then heated again to be removed. You can apply white school glue in a pattern, allow it to dry, and then apply the dye of your choice either with a paintbrush or a spray bottle.

Let the dye set for as long as the manufacturer's directions tell you to, then rinse your fabric in cold water to remove the glue. Set the color as explained by the manufacturer (usually by washing with soap and hot water) and then let dry.

You can try painting your fabric instead of dying it. You may be wondering what the difference is between fabric paint and fabric dye. Well, the main difference is how it interacts with the

WHAT'S HOT

▶ There are so many different things you can do with tie dye. From wild color combinations to creative designs, you can personalize almost anything! Tie dye makes a fun activity for a children's birthday party, a family reunion, or a community fundraiser. For more great tie dye tips and project ideas, visit my About.com site: http://about.com/family crafts/tiedye.

fabric. Fabric dyes change the color of the entire piece of fabric. Fabric paint sits on the surface of the fabric and only adds color to the spot where it is applied.

You can apply fabric paint in many ways. Several of them come in small bottles with a pointed tip, so you can write or draw directly from the bottle. You can also use a paintbrush, or make designs on fabric using fingers, stamps, sponges, or anything else you can make a print with. When my boys were young, they loved making a race-car shirt by painting the tires of a toy car with fabric paint and "driving" it over a shirt.

There are a few things you should keep in mind when using fabric paints. First of all, they are pretty thick, so sometimes they take more than 24 hours to dry. Also, because they are so thick, sometimes they end up being stiff on your fabric, especially if you are painting large areas. Test small areas if you have any doubts about how a fabric paint will feel once dry. Heat will make some fabric paint soften, causing designs to stick together in a hot dryer.

Why not decorate your fabric items using crayons or markers! Buy some fabric crayons or fabric markers, and you can make several designer-like articles of clothing and even household decorations!

Fabric markers are great for drawing detailed pictures and for experimenting with shading and blending. Read the packaging, because some manufacturers suggest you set the design with heat once you are done drawing it. Make sure you buy markers specially designed for working with fabric. You should find them by the fabric paints at the craft store. Pens that are simply marked as having "permanent ink" will not hold up well to several washings.

You can choose between two different kinds of fabric crayons. The first are Pentel Fabric Fun Crayons. These are nontoxic,

TOOLS YOU NEED

▶ If you want to try your hand at fabric dying without a lot of preparation or the mess that comes with dying, you might want to try Simply Spray fabric-dye products (www.simplyspray.com). The concept is simple—fabric dye in a can that is used like regular spray paint, and it seems very easy to use. They have a product line for clothing, for use with stencils, and also for use with upholstery.

intense colors in soft stick form and are much like using pastels. You can color directly on the fabric, and the nice thing about these is that if you don't like the picture, you can wash it out. The directions say that the pictures you draw are not permanent until you set them with the heat of an iron.

The second kind of fabric crayons are used a little differently than the Pentel Fabric Fun Crayons. These look the same as regular coloring crayons, except you may notice the color looks a little duller. Instead of coloring directly on the fabric, you create your own iron-on transfer. You draw/color your picture onto a white piece of paper, keeping in mind that everything will be transferred in reverse. The color will appear duller on the paper. If you want darker areas, you are better off applying multiple layers of color, because pressing too hard may give your picture a grainy appearance.

Once you get your picture how you want it, lightly dust the paper to brush away any specks of crayon that you don't want to transfer. You should lay your paper picture-side-down on a clean, pressed, light-colored piece of fabric or clothing. The transfer will work best on synthetic fabrics or a synthetic blend. Carefully press the design for as long as the package says. Don't rub, because if the paper shifts the design might smear. Once your design is heat set with the iron it will be permanent and machine washable.

Adding Flair to Your Wardrobe

Of course, you can use fabric dyes, paints, markers, and crayons to customize your clothing, but there are plenty of other options also. You can use a variety of products and techniques to embellish your shirts, jeans, shoes, hats, and more. Besides sewing on embellishments, you can easily find glue that is specially made for attaching items to fabric. Experiment by gluing or sewing on any of these embellishment items:

ASK YOUR GUIDE

Can I use ordinary coloring crayons to add color and detail to clothes?

▶ From what I have read, the answer to this question is yes. Basically, you color right on the fabric and then set the color with the heat from an iron (cover the colored area with paper). The up side is that there are many more colors to choose from; the down side is the colors are not as bright as with the transfer method. Experiment and see which way you like best.

- Beads
- Buttons
- Sequins
- Ribbon
- Cording
- Lace
- Fringe
- Wiggle eyes
- Rick-rack
- Fabric scraps
- Fur
- Tassels

You can also try other techniques. While some of these embellishing methods might require special tools, most can be accomplished with supplies you already have.

You can create your own iron-on transfers. One of the simplest ways is to use the fabric crayons we talked about a bit earlier in this chapter. All ages can have great success with this method, as long as an adult deals with the ironing. You can also make nice-quality iron-on transfers using your computer, photographs or graphics, an iron, and iron-on transfer paper.

While you should read the instructions for whatever brand of iron-on transfer paper you buy, most of the steps are similar.

1. Find the image you want to use. If it is not already in your computer, scan or download it. Make sure it is reversed! The image should look backwards when it is printed, so it will be the right way once it is ironed onto the fabric.
2. Print a test page first, making sure it fits your paper and your fabric. If you are happy with the test page, load the

ELSEWHERE ON THE WEB

▶ While you can use any graphics program on your computer to print photos and clip art onto iron-on transfers, you may want to try a computer program made especially for making these transfers. There are several on the market, but why not try one for free? Drop by the Hanes Web site (www.hanes2u.com) and give the free version of their software a test drive. There is even extra clip art you can download.

iron-on transfer paper into your printer. Check your printer settings; some have a setting for iron-on transfer paper. If yours doesn't, set your printer for high-quality glossy paper. Print your image.

3. Carefully remove the iron-on transfer sheet from your printer and allow the ink to dry completely. Do not handle the paper while the ink is drying. Trim around your design if necessary.

4. Turn your iron to the hottest setting and make sure it is set to NO STEAM. Lay a pillowcase or dishtowel down on a hard surface that is safe to iron on (do not using an ironing board). Place the object you are embellishing onto the dishtowel or pillowcase and press to make a nice, smooth surface to transfer your design to. Let cool.

5. Lay the fabric item on top of the surface you prepared. Then lay your transfer picture-side-down onto your fabric in the desired position. Press all areas of the paper with the iron, making sure you follow the manufacturer's time guidelines. Make sure your transfer paper does not move while you are pressing it.

6. Carefully peel off the paper while it is warm, using the iron on any spots that stick. Make sure you follow the manufacturer's suggestions for machine washing your iron-on transfer and it should last you for quite a while!

You can add some sparkle to your clothes using rhinestones. The popularity of embellishing with rhinestones is timeless, and the possibilities are endless! You can create everything from simple designs to elaborate pictures. All it takes is some flat-backed rhinestones and glue, needle and thread, heat, or a setting tool. The method you use will depend on the project and the rhinestones you purchase.

WHAT'S HOT

▶ Adding extra sparkle and shine to clothing is popular and fun, especially adding fancy studs to jeans and shiny rhinestones to shirts. You can add both of these, and more, using special heat tools, sometimes referred to as hot-fix applicators. The Kandi Kane (www.kandicorp.com) is one of the more popular tools, probably due to the fact that it can be used with a variety of applicator tips for special rhinestones, studs, crystals, and pearls.

- **Glue:** The simplest method is to glue your rhinestones onto your fabric item. You should use a glue made especially for bonding nonporous items to porous items, such as Gem-Tac. Simply dab a small amount of glue, proportionate to the size of your rhinestone, onto your fabric. Carefully place the rhinestone—a set of tweezers works well—onto the glue, making sure there is just enough glue to come up and surround the edge of the rhinestone. Let the glue dry completely, and then you can wash and wear your item.
- **Needle and thread:** You can find special rhinestones that have two holes in them that are big enough for a needle and thread to fit through. Simply sew these rhinestones onto anything you like.
- **Heat:** You can find rhinestones with special heat-sensitive glue on the back. These are applied to surfaces using heat from either a household iron or a special tool. When the glue on the back of the rhinestone is heated it melts and "grabs" onto the surface you are applying it to.
  - ▶ To use an iron, lay your fabric item onto your hard ironing surface. Place your heat-sensitive rhinestones, glue side down, in the desired pattern onto your fabric item. Carefully lay a thin cloth or pressing sheet over the rhinestones. Press with a hot iron. Check the manufacturer's label for heat settings and pressing times. Let the item cool completely before you move it.
  - ▶ Using a special rhinestone heat tool is definitely easier than using a household iron. You attach the rhinestones one at a time so you don't have to worry about shifting and slipping. I would suggest trying this craft with an iron first, and if it's something you plan on doing more often, invest in a special rhinestone-setting heat tool.

- **Setting Tool:** This tool is fairly easy to use, and the only other things you need are a rhinestone and a setting. The setting has prongs that grab onto the rhinestone. The prongs get bent either around the top of the rhinestone, up through the fabric in a jewel-type setting, or the setting looks like a ring that sits over the top of the rhinestone and the prongs grab onto and hold the fabric underneath.

You can create your own appliqués to decorate anything made of fabric. Simply stated, appliqué involves cutting a shape out of one fabric and sewing that shape onto another fabric. If you ask any quilter or sewing enthusiast, they will tell you that all of the different methods used to add appliqué designs to garments and other fabric items can fill a book by themselves. However, I will explain just the basics, and they can be modified and adjusted to suit the tastes of even the most advanced crafters.

The first thing you usually need for appliquéing is a pattern. This can be from a purchased pattern, coloring book, or even a hand-drawn design. It's easiest to transfer each aspect of your pattern separately onto paper-backed, fusible webbing by tracing it. However, be aware that your pattern will be reversed once it is ironed onto your fabric, so everything should be drawn and written backward. The traced pieces can then be ironed onto the back side of the fabric. Once the paper cools, you can cut out the design, remove the paper backing, and iron the design fabric onto your fabric item.

If your fabric item will be heavily used and/or frequently washed, such as an article of clothing or a table cloth, secure the edges of your appliqué using a tight zigzag stitch on a sewing machine, or by tracing the outline with dimensional fabric paint. If the item will not be washed or used as often, you can leave it as-is, or hand-sew fancy stitches around the edges.

▶ Fusible webbing is a very useful tool when working with wearables. They are a glue- or plastic-based material that is either sandwiched between paper or has paper on one side. They are used to attach pieces of fabric, usually appliqué-pattern pieces, to the fabric base. Before being ironed onto the fabric, the webbing is usually see-through, but becomes invisible once heat is applied. Fusible web can be purchased by the yard, in sheet form, or in rolls.

Eyelets and grommets make unique and useful embellishments. Grommets and eyelets are rings, usually metal, that are inserted into a hole made through another material—usually paper or fabric. They may be used to reinforce the hole or simply for decorative purposes. These days, eyelets are a popular design element used in scrapbooking, but they can also be used as a design element when working with fabric.

While some people think that eyelets and grommets are the same thing, grommets are usually bigger, have a wider rim, and look more industrial than eyelets. Grommets are usually used for additional holding strength in high-stress applications such as tents, banners, and flags. Eyelets are usually the first choice when it comes to garments, hats, shoes, and paper projects. So, which one is right for you? It all depends on your personal preferences and the project at hand.

The tools needed to apply eyelets and grommets are similar, one is just a little bigger than the other. First, you need either a hole punch or a craft knife to make a small hole in your fabric. You then poke the eyelet or grommet (usually with a washer) through the hole, and then tap a setter using a small hammer or rubber mallet.

Hats and Scarves

During the right season you can usually find knit stocking caps and scarves at very affordable prices. This is a great time to stock up so you have a nice supply on hand for embellishing. Appliqué techniques or dimensional fabric paint are great choices for personalizing knit hats and scarves. Plain baseball-type caps are extra special when you add your own personal touches, such as fabric paint, rhinestones, or just about any other embellishing technique. You can also find a variety of plain cloth, plastic, or craft-foam visors at your local craft store. All of these make wonderful bases for wearable masterpieces. You can also make your own hats and scarves using the following ideas.

▶ Since we are talking about wearables, I would like to introduce you to a product I discovered recently. It's called SunGuard (www.sunguardsunprotection.com). It is a revolutionary laundry aid that washes sun protection into your clothing. What does this mean? It means that it helps to block more than 96 percent of the sun's harmful ultraviolet (UV) rays from reaching your skin. Sun block built into your clothing. Cool!

Fleece Hat

Fleece is a great fabric for craft projects. It's soft and flexible and comes in so many colors and prints! This simple hat is a great project for kids—or you can make one for that special kid in your life.

26" × 26" piece of fleece (approximate, read the measurement directions below)
Scissors
Needle and thread

1. Measure around the head of the person who will wear the hat, then add 1" to the measurement. Cut a piece of fleece as long as your measurement, plus the 1" by about 26". Save your scraps!

2. Lay the fleece on your work surface. Fold up one side so your piece will be 26" tall by half the width of the measured head plus 1". Line up both long edges. If your fleece has a right side, make sure the right side is in when you fold your fleece.

3. Sew these long edges together, forming a long tube, leaving about ½" seam allowance. You can easily sew this by hand using a needle and thread and a straight stitch. You can also sew this on a machine if you like.

4. Now fold up one end of the tube and match up the two raw edges. The raw edges of the seam you just sewed should be on the inside. You should now be able to fit the folded edge on your head and the raw edges will stick up.

5. Find or cut a piece of fleece about 2" × 8". This part is easier if you put the hat on someone else's head. Now, gather the raw edges along the top of your hat and tie the 8" piece of fleece around it like a ponytail.

ELSEWHERE ON THE WEB

▶ If you want to take fabric dying a step further, you can experiment with dying using natural materials. Do you believe that the source for natural dyes can be found right in your own back yard? Roots, nuts, and flowers are just a few common natural ways to get many colors. Yellow, orange, blue, red, green, brown, and gray are also available. Go ahead, experiment! Find directions here: www.pioneerthinking.com/naturaldyes.html.

6. Finally, use the scissors and cut strips 1" wide in the raw edges to make it look like a big pom-pom on top of your hat. Trim the fringes down so they are 3" to 4" long.

Homemade Scarf

Make a scarf to match your hat, as a special gift, or even to show your school spirit!

¼ yard of fleece, flannel, or other heavy fabric
Masking tape
Scissors

1. Trim your piece of fabric to measure approximately 9" × 52". This is usually easier using a straight-edge ruler and rotary cutter, if you have one.
2. From one of the 9" ends, measure up about 4" from the bottom edge and mark this line with a piece of masking tape running the whole 9" width of the fabric.
3. Cut slits in the fabric from the end up to the piece of tape, about every 1", so you end up with fringe that is 4" long. Repeat this on the other end.
4. Carefully remove the masking tape.
5. You can wear the scarf like this or embellish as desired. Try cutting your initials out of contrasting pieces of fabric and gluing them near the fringe ends, or write your entire name using dimensional fabric paint. How about embellishing the entire scarf with a variety of buttons or by simply gluing small pom-poms to the ends of the fringe?

▶ There is a large selection of fancy trims on the market these days. You can use them to decorate any wearables, or for a variety of other projects, such as card making and scrapbooking. Experiment with different trims such as those with beads, sequins, pom-poms, tassels, and fringe. They can be applied using glue or by sewing them on. Most of all, they add a decorative touch to everything!

For Your Hands and Feet

When embellishing your wearables, don't forget about your hands and feet. Many of the coloring and embellishing ideas would work well for shoes, slippers, mittens, and gloves. For example, you can use dimensional paint to personalize a pair of white canvas tennis shoes, and embellish them with beads, buttons, or rhinestones. And don't forget to add a pair of tie-dyed shoelaces made the same way you would a shirt. You can also make a matching pair of gloves or mittens. For some fancy fingers, use shiny fabric paint to color the tips of your glove fingers to look like painted fingernails. Use silver or gold fabric paint and rhinestones to draw beautiful rings and bracelets on your glove.

Fleece Mittens

If you made a fleece hat and scarf, why not keep working with the fleece and make some matching mittens.

¼ yard of fleece	Paper
Pencil	Scissors
Straight pins	Needle and thread

1. Put a piece of paper down on your work surface and lay your hand on top of it, fingers together. Starting about 1" below your wrist, trace around your hand to create a mitten pattern. Cut out your pattern, staying about ½" outside of the line you drew to give you enough room for a seam allowance.
2. Use your pattern to cut out four pieces of fleece to make your mittens.
3. Pin two of the mitten pieces together, lining up all edges evenly. Repeat for the other set of mitten pieces.

WHAT'S HOT

▶ You can spend a fortune on designer purses and handbags. Instead, why not create your own designer purses and handbags using a variety of supplies and techniques? You can make everything from a sequined handbag to a simple coin purse—or how about making a purse using juice-box pouches, duct tape, or placemats! You can choose from several free patterns featured at this site: http://about.com/familycrafts/purseswallets.

Sewn mittens

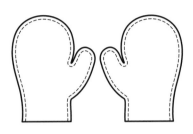

4. Use your needle and thread and a straight stitch, or a sewing machine, to sew your mitten-edges together. Begin at the wrist and sew around all edges, leaving the wrist-edge open.
5. Turn your mittens right side out and they are ready to wear! You may need to trim the wrist edge of the mitten so they are even. Embellish your mittens and enjoy!

Non-Slip Slipper Socks

This project is quick, easy, and would make a great craft for a slumber party for a group of kids.

Heavy socks
Puffy fabric paint

1. Lay the socks flat on your work surface so that the bottom side is up.
2. Now, simply use the puffy fabric paint to make dots, lines, or other shapes on the bottom of the sock. This will transform the ordinary socks into socks with a non-skid bottom.
3. Depending on how thick the paint is applied, the designs may take several hours to dry.
4. Once the bottoms are dry, you can decorate the top of the sock if you want. Wear and enjoy.

Tote Bags and Purses

These days you can usually find a large selection of plain canvas totes and other bags at your local craft store. You can decorate these using any of the methods shared here. If you want to go one step further, you can make your own tote bags and purses.

Bandana Backpack

With the wide variety of colorful bandanas available these days, the hardest part of this project might be picking only two!

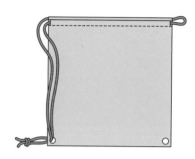

2 bandanas of the same size	4 yards of cording
Needle and thread	2 grommets and setting tool
Straight pins	Scissors

1. Fold one edge of each bandana down 1", right-sides-out, and pin to secure. Sew along the edge to make a tube-like casing for the cording. Make sure you leave each end open.
2. Now lay both bandanas down on your work surface on top of each other, right sides together. Make sure the casing edges you made are lined up evenly. Pin the two bandanas together.
3. Using about ¼" seam allowance, start just below the casing on one side and sew around three edges, stopping just before the casing on the other side. Make sure you don't sew the casing openings closed.
4. Turn the bag right side out.
5. Using the directions that come with the grommet-setting tool, set a grommet in each bottom corner (the corners opposite the casing).
6. Cut your piece of cording into two separate 2-yard pieces.
7. Feed 1 end of the cording through one of the grommets, pull it up the side of the bag, and thread it through one of the tube-like casings. Now thread it through the other tube-like casing, this time starting from the side nearest where your cording just came out of the other casing. Now feed this end back through the same grommet from the same side you threaded it out of. Tie the ends by holding them evenly and tying an overhand knot.

8. Repeat this process to add cord through the other side.
9. You can now pull the top of the bag shut by pulling on the cords, and the cord can be worn over both shoulders.

Recycled Blue-Jean Tote Bag

You can transform old blue jeans into a fashionable tote bag. This is much easier than it sounds, and can be made in just an hour or two. The only thing you have to watch for is that the belt loops are in good shape.

Pair of jeans	Straight pins
Needle and thread	Scissors

1. Lay the jeans flat on your work surface and cut off each leg. From one of the legs, cut two strips about 4" × 24".
2. Turn the jeans inside out and pin together both of the openings you just cut.
3. Leaving about ½" seam allowance, stitch the openings closed starting on one side, stitching across the crotch area, and then stitching across the other opening.
4. Turn your new blue-jean tote bag right-side-out. Iron if desired.
5. Sew the two 4" × 24" strips together, using ½" seam allowance, so you have a strip that is approximately 4" × 47".
6. Fold the strip in half lengthwise, right sides together. Line up the long edges and sew the entire length using about ½" seam allowance to form a long tube.
7. Turn this tube right side out. Iron if desired. This will be your strap.
8. Slip one end of your strap into the belt loop on one side of the jeans, then thread that same end through the belt loop on the opposite side of the jeans. Tie or sew the two ends together.
9. Your strap is now ready, and you can embellish if desired.

Get Linked

If you like the idea of displaying your craft projects by wearing them and want even more ideas, check out these resources:

PICTURES OF CHAPTER 7 CRAFTS

Visit the URL below to see colored photos of all of the craft projects shared in this chapter. You can also share photos or crafts you've completed.

http://about.com/familycrafts/chapter7

WEARABLES AND ACCESSORIES

Find out how you can use many creative techniques and supplies to make and decorate your own clothing, jewelry, and other items you can wear.

http://about.com/familycrafts/wearables

Chapter 8

Educational Crafts

Science

If you think about it, science plays a big part in some craft projects. When you mix up a batch of clay or try your hand at dying fabric, you are dabbling in science! When you make the recipe for bubbles and go outside to blow them, the kids may not know it, but that is science at work. While you are doing these activities, don't flood them with scientific facts and findings. Instead, ask them simple questions and let them ask you questions. Get them thinking about it, and then you can even help them do a little research.

While many of the projects in this book may include some scientific properties, here are a few to get you started. Of course, with any of these crafty "experiments" there should be plenty of adult supervision.

Fossil Fun

A long time ago, plants, bugs, and animals left their impressions in soft mud, which dried out, got buried, and eventually became rock. These rocks are called fossils. Much of what we know about plants and animals that lived long ago was discovered by scientists who studied fossils. Since it takes more years than we can count to create real fossils, we can make fun fossil prints using these instructions.

½ cup flour	½ cup used coffee grounds
¼ cup salt	¼ cup sand
Water	Fossil objects (sea shells, plastic dinosaurs, or other small objects)

1. First mix together all of the dry ingredients.
2. Add the water a little at a time until you have a thick dough. You don't want it to crumble, but you also don't want it too wet and sticky.
3. Flatten your dough on your work surface so it is about 1" thick.
4. Carefully press and remove your fossil objects into your clay until you get a nice impression.
5. Let your clay fossil dry completely before you move it. This can take a few days, depending on the thickness of your project and the humidity.
6. If you like, instead of making fossil prints, you can form a rock with your dough and hide a small fossil object inside. Once it dries (leave for several days) you can break it open and see what kind of shape your object leaves.

Grow Some Crystals

If you do some research, you will find that there are a large variety of "recipes" for growing your own crystals. Do some experimenting and compare how crystals made from different ingredients are different and alike. I picked this recipe to share simply because it uses ingredients you either have in your home or that you can find in your local grocery store.

½ cup of water
2+ tablespoons of alum powder (found in the spice section at the grocery store)
Food coloring
Baby-food jar
Paper towel

1. Put the water into a microwave-safe container. Heat in the microwave on high for 1½ minutes.
2. Slowly add the alum to the water, stirring to dissolve. Keep adding the alum, a little at a time, until it does not dissolve anymore. Add food coloring if desired. Let this mixture settle for a minute or two.
3. Carefully empty the alum and water mixture into the baby-food jar, making sure no undissolved alum gets into the jar.
4. Put the jar someplace where it will not be disturbed for a few days, loosely covering it with a piece of paper towel to keep dust out.
5. Watch your jar carefully for the next few days, but make sure it doesn't get moved! After about three days, or when the crystals are the desired size, carefully pour off the water, remove your crystals, and set them out on a paper towel to dry.

ELSEWHERE ON THE WEB

▶ Did you know you can use techniques similar to the ones shared here for crystal making to make your own rock candy? You hang a string in the jar and, as the water evaporates, the resulting sugar crystals form on the string. The shapes that they form reflect the shape of individual sugar crystals. Best of all, this simple mixture of sugar and water can produce yummy crystals you can really eat. You can find a recipe here: www.sciencebob. com/experiments/rockcandy. html.

6. Make more crystals, experimenting with different colors, times, and even recipes. Try looking at them under a magnifying glass or a microscope.

Make a Volcano

A fun lesson in chemical reactions is making your own miniature volcano that will really erupt. This is a small volcano, but its eruption will still be grand! If you want a bigger volcano, you can use a 2-liter bottle and make a paper mache mountain! When you are ready for your volcano to erupt, take it outside or in a well-protected area, as it will be messy!

Masking tape	2 small, disposable cups
Paper plate	Clay
1 tablespoon warm water	Liquid dishwashing soap
Food coloring	1 tablespoon of baking soda
Vinegar	

1. Use the masking tape to attach the disposable cup to the center of the paper plate.
2. Use clay to form a mountain on the plate around the cup. You can purchase modeling clay or mix up a batch of clay from Chapter 2 (my favorite for this project is the No-Cook Play Clay on page 27). Depending on which recipe you choose, you may need to mix up a double batch. You want your mountain to completely cover the side of the cup. The hole in the cup will be the crater where the lava comes out, so be careful to not get any clay in it. You may want to let the clay dry, but you don't have to.
3. Now prepare for your eruption! First, measure the water into your volcano crater. Add three to four drops of dishwashing

TOOLS YOU NEED

▶ If you and your child want to learn more about volcanoes, the Volcano World site is a wonderful tool to use: http://volcano.und.edu. "Wow!" is all I can say. Besides the stuff you would expect to find, such as volcano FAQs and pictures, there is so much more. The section I found most fascinating is the page that lists the most current eruptions that also includes commentary and photos.

soap and three to four drops of food coloring. Stir in the baking soda.

4. Fill the other small disposable cup about ⅓ full of vinegar.
5. Quickly pour the vinegar into your volcano crater, step back, and watch your volcano's bubbly eruption!

Windsock

Most of us have seen windsocks hanging in backyards and on patios. While these windsocks are more for decorative purposes, windsocks are used by scientists and even airplane pilots to find out the direction and strength of the wind. Using these directions, you can make your own windsock so you can tell with a glance how the wind is blowing.

Long-shirt sleeve or lightweight pant leg
Wire hanger or heavy-gauge wire
Weight
String
Duct or masking tape
Needle and thread
Straight pins
Scissors
Wire cutters

1. Cut your sleeve or pant leg so it is even along the top edge. Measure the circumference of the cut edge.
2. Use the wire cutter to cut a piece of hanger or heavy wire to that same measurement, plus 2". Twist the last 1" of each end of the hanger piece or wire to form a circle.
3. Find a small rock, about 1" in diameter, or use a fishing weight or large metal washer. Use the tape to attach the rock to your wire hoop, covering the spot where both wires are twisted

▶ Weather is something that is always on people's minds. It impacts so many areas of our life that kids can't help but be curious about it. That is why learning about weather is a great way to get kids involved with science. Kids can spend hours exploring weather-related topics such as hurricanes, tornadoes, clouds, lightning, earthquakes, and even optical illusions. While they are learning more about these natural occurrences, they can even make weather-related crafts: http://about.com/familycrafts/weather.

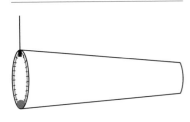

together. The weight will help keep the windsock facing into the wind.

4. Cut a piece of string about 2' long and tie it to the wire hoop opposite the rock.
5. Now, place the wire into the cut end of the sleeve, folding over about ½". Use the straight pins to hold the sleeve in place.
6. Use the needle and thread to sew the sleeve in place. You can cover the rock, but make sure the string end is loose.
7. Tie the end of the string onto a branch or other spot where it can move freely. You can now watch your windsock blow. Use a compass to find which way the wind is blowing!

Math

Some kids may not agree, but math is a very important part of life. We use math to buy groceries, set a wrist watch, bake cookies, keep score at a sporting event, and many other things. Many of these things can be used as a math lesson without kids even knowing it. There are also many creative ways to reinforce math skills.

Sorting Sticks

Work together with your child to create this fun activity that will help with math skills such as sorting, counting, addition, subtraction, and other concepts. I bet you can think of even more game ideas than what I have included here!

Several craft sticks
Paint
Clear acrylic spray
Recycled jar, potato-chip container, etc. (or any container that will hold several craft sticks)

1. The number of craft sticks you want will depend on the number of concepts you want to work on. For the youngest kids, ten sticks will do; as they master that, you can add more.

2. Have the kids paint the craft sticks. Offer them four different colors of paint and have them paint their sticks each a solid color. They should paint one side of the stick, allow it to dry and then paint the other side. Instruct them to color at least one stick each color, but preferably paint each color onto a different number of sticks. For example, one red stick, two blue sticks, three yellow sticks, and four green sticks. If kids want different combinations, that is fine too.

3. Once all of the paint is dry, take the sticks outside or to a well-ventilated area and spray them with clear acrylic spray. Let one side dry and then spray the other. This will protect the sticks from chipping and scratching.

4. While the kids are waiting for the sticks to dry, they can paint or decorate the recycled container.

5. The sticks should all be put into the container. You will use the container for playing some games and also for storage.

6. Kids can practice a variety of math skills using these sticks: they can sort the sticks by color; count them; add or subtract different colors/numbers (for example, "How much is red plus blue?"); place the piles of sticks in order from fewest to most; count by twos; separate the piles by even or odd numbers; and so on.

Learning about Time

These days it is a little harder to teach kids about telling time and reading a clock, simply because digital clocks are more common than analog clocks. This craft can help them learn how to read a clock and about different times of day.

ELSEWHERE ON THE WEB

▶ For a ton of math fun for kids, both online and offline, check out Math Cat's site at www.mathcats.com. This site has so much to offer that your kids will spend hours here! They can start out by reading math news, interesting number stories, explore the math art gallery, and even look at photos featuring human-body geometry. And when your kids are done with all of that, they can try their hand at several craft projects.

▶ If you really want to teach time, you can have your child help you make a real clock. Clock movements can be bought at any craft store or online for less than $10, and they are fairly easy to make! For the most part, you simply need a hole about ½" in diameter, in an object that the clock movement mechanism can fit through. You can drill a hole in almost anything to create a unique clock.

Paper plate
Crayons or markers
Number stickers (1 through 12)
Scrap piece of colored construction paper or cardstock
Poster board or large piece of cardstock
Paper brad (brass paper fastener)
Magazines and/or pictures printed from computer
Glue stick
Scissors

1. Allow kids to color the face of their clock (paper plate) with crayons or markers if desired. Have them use the stickers to place the correct number in the appropriate spots on the clock face.
2. Draw two hands (arrows) for the clock on colored paper or cardstock, one a little smaller than the other. Have the kids cut them out.
3. Glue the paper-plate clock face to the center of the poster board using the glue stick.
4. Push the ends of both clock hands onto the pointed ends of the paper brad, and then poke the paper brad through the center of the paper-plate clock face, also going all of the way through the poster board. The paper brad should be loose enough so that the clock hands can move around freely. It may be helpful to poke a small hole first using a craft knife.
5. The clock is now ready to use to practice telling time. Show your child how the hands on the clock move, and how the numbers on the clock represent a time of day.
6. Use pictures cut from magazines or computer-generated pictures to represent different activities that happen daily, such as wake-up time, lunch time, play time, story time, etc., and glue these pictures on the poster board around the clock.

Making Shapes

This is a fun painting activity that you can use to discuss geometric shapes with kids. Find objects that represent a variety of different shapes. Besides circles, squares, rectangles, and triangles, offer shapes such as a hexagon (six sides), octagon (eight sides), diamond, oval, and any other shapes you want to show them.

> Paper
> Acrylic or tempera paint
> Styrofoam meat tray, Styrofoam plate, or other shallow
>   container
> Stamp objects (see below)

1. Gather together a variety of items you can use to stamp shapes onto the paper. You can find objects that offer basic shapes in a variety of sizes, or you can also make your own stamps using sponges or potatoes.
2. Give the child a piece of paper.
3. Pour paint into a shallow container. Use a different container for each color of paint.
4. Show the child how to dip the stamp into the paint and press it onto the paper.
5. Let your child experiment with different colors and shapes. If they want, let them use a sheet of paper for each shape, color, or whatever they want. Discuss the different shapes and point out other places you may see these shapes.

3-Dimensional Numbers

These are great number pictures you can hang around the house for decoration and help with recognition. Hang the numbers low enough so

ASK YOUR GUIDE

How can I make my own sponge shapes for painting?

▶ You can simply buy cheap household sponges and cut out whatever shapes you like, but I would suggest giving Miracle Sponges a try! A Miracle Sponge is a sponge that is thinly compressed to resemble a piece of paper. You can easily draw your design on the 8" × 11" sheet and cut it out. Once water is added, the sponge swells to the size of a normal sponge.

the child can touch the different objects. Because of the small objects used in this craft, it is not recommended for kids who still put things in their mouths.

Heavy poster board	Crayons or markers
Craft glue	Small objects (suggestions below)
Scissors	

1. Cut large numbers 1 through 9 out of heavy poster board. You want the numbers to be about 8" to 9" tall. You can easily find templates online or use a word-processing program on your computer to make numbers using a large font size.
2. Have the child practice writing the number on each cutout. They can also color on it using crayons and markers.
3. Gather small objects you can have the child glue on the numbers, such as beads, buttons, small pom-poms, cereal, noodles, paper clips, pebbles, etc.
4. Let the kids glue the corresponding number of items on each cut-out number.

Language Arts

Technically, language arts is a school subject that focuses on listening, reading, writing, and speaking skills. We can use crafts to practice and reinforce these skills, starting with the most basic of these skills: learning the alphabet!

Alphabet Lacing Cards

Kids young and old will have fun lacing around these craft-foam letters. Older kids may like the idea of spelling out their names using laced letters and hanging them on their bedroom walls, while younger kids will

▶ One of the more popular educational-craft sections on my Web site features craft projects related to the alphabet. There are a variety of free projects, including directions for making your own paper alphabet blocks with an included printable template, a collection of alphabet-related, beaded safety-pin patterns, printable coloring book pages, and even a tasty alphabet snack recipe! These ideas can be found here: http://about.com/familycrafts/alphabet.

really benefit from working with letter recognition. If your child can do all of the preparations, encourage him to do so. For younger kids, you can prepare the craft-foam letters and cut the yarn.

Craft foam   Yarn, ribbon, cording, or plastic lace
Scissors   Clear cellophane or masking tape
Hole puncher

1. Make your craft-foam letters. You can use these printable letters as templates: http://about.com/familycrafts/alphapages. Simply print them, trace them onto the craft foam, and cut them out.
2. Use the hole puncher to make holes around the outside edge of each letter, about 1" apart.
3. Cut a piece of yarn, ribbon, etc. about 3' long. Tie one end onto the craft-foam letter, then wrap the other end with a small piece of tape to make it easier to thread through the holes.
4. The alphabet lacing cards can now be used over and over again. Encourage kids to lace the yarn through the holes using different techniques, or to use a few different pieces of yarn, etc. Have them use their creativity!

Poetry Magnets

You can buy these magnetic words at stores for big bucks or you can spend a few dollars and a little time and make your own magnetic poetry. You can create these for any age. For young kids, make bigger magnets or simple letters and words, you can also make letters and endings, such as "at," "an," "en," and so on, so that two magnets can be put together to make a word. Let older kids write their own words. They can use names of family and friends, popular places, current slang terms, plus plenty of filler words such as "the," "and," "is," and so on.

ELSEWHERE ON THE WEB

▶ If you want to play with some virtual magnetic poetry, check out this page: www.magneticpoetry.com. You can browse the products, including magnetic poetry stepping-stone kits, but make sure you take some time to visit their Play page. If you opt to choose a kit, you can play with artist-, genius-, poet-, office-, romance-, or gardener-themed poetry. If you choose the Play Online option, the themes to choose from include friends, horses, Shakespeare, dog lover, and more.

Inkjet magnetic sheets   Computer paper
Candy tin (such as Altoids)   Paint
Clear acrylic spray   Scissors

1. Type up your custom word list (or have your child type it) using my suggestions or your own ideas. Double space the lines and leave enough space between words so you can cut them out easily. Don't forget to add plenty of common nouns, verbs, pronouns, and conjunctions to your word list.
2. Once the word list is ready, print a test page on regular paper and proofread it. If it looks good, print it out on the magnet sheet.
3. Let the ink dry, then spray your magnet sheet with a few light coats of the clear acrylic spray, letting it dry between coats.
4. While you are waiting for your magnet sheet to dry, have your child paint the candy tin however she likes. Spray the dry tin with a few coats of clear acrylic spray.
5. Now you can use the scissors to carefully cut out the words and/or letters. Cut out a row first, and then each individual word or letter.
6. The words and/or letter can be used on a refrigerator, locker, or even a cookie sheet. You can store your magnets in the tin or even stick letters to it.

Write Your Own Story Book

This project can be adjusted to fit almost all ages. The idea is to have your child create her own picture book. First she finds the pictures and then she writes the story.

Construction paper   White paper
Ribbon   Magazines

▶ To help kids with everything from mathematical functions to the alphabet, why not make a portable flashcard set? All you need is some index cards cut in half, a marker, a hole puncher, and a clip-on key ring. Simply write whatever it is they are working on onto the index cards, punch a hole in the corner of each card, and thread them onto the key ring. Now your child can take their flashcards with them wherever they go.

Glue stick   Hole puncher
Scissors

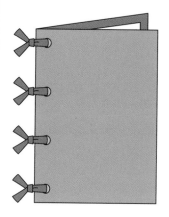

Tie the pages of the book together using ribbon

1. Have your child fold a piece of construction paper in half to form the book cover and back.
2. Decide how many pages the book should have. Take half that number of papers and fold them in half. Slip them in the construction-paper book cover.
3. Use the hole puncher and make four sets of holes down the folded side of the book for the binding.
4. Cut four pieces of ribbon about 6" long. Push a piece of ribbon through each set of holes and tie them in a bow to hold your book pages together.
5. Now your child can start to make her book! She can start out by writing the story, spreading it out over all of the pages. Make sure she leaves plenty of room for pictures.
6. Once the story is done, have your child thumb through magazines and find pictures that will go with her story. She should glue the pictures in the book using the glue stick. The book is now ready to read and share.
7. If your child wants a bigger challenge or does not know what to write about, suggest finding the pictures for the story first. Just make sure your child leaves plenty of room to write the story when the pictures are glued in.

Social Studies

This topic can cover subjects such as geography, current events, history, cultures, community, and even holidays. It pretty much encompasses any subject related to human society, past and present. While you can find a large selection of multicultural, historical, and other related crafts online on my About.com site, here are a few basics to get you started.

About-My-Community Scrapbook

Have your child decorate a plain three-ring binder, composition book, or notebook to use as a tool to help her learn about different places and people in her community, along with history, special events, and community celebrations.

Three-ring binder	Cardstock
Markers	Magazines
Glue stick	Hole punch
Scissors	

1. Have your child decorate the three-ring binder however she wants. One idea is to cover it with photos from around your neighborhood or town and then personalize it with markers.
2. You can make the cardstock pages fit in your book by punching three holes in the side of each piece where the binder rings will fit through. (You want to use cardstock because it will hold up better to glue.)
3. Now your child can start to make her book! Talk about different community workers such as police officers, firefighters, mail carriers, doctors, and anyone else who serves the people in their community. Page through a variety of magazines and find pictures related to different community workers and cut them out. Make a page for each job and make a collage using the pictures you found.
4. You can also plan visits to places such as fire stations, police stations, post offices, restaurants, and so on. Have your child take pictures or make drawings related to what she sees. Add these to the three-ring binder.

5. Another idea well suited to older kids is to interview different neighbors and take pictures of them and their home to include in your book.

Make a Flag

Explain to your child that every country has its own unique flag. While many flags use similar colors and shapes, each country's flag uses colors and symbols in a different way, and each has special meaning to the people of the country. For example, you can explain to them that the flag of the United States consists of thirteen equal horizontal stripes of red alternating with white, with a blue rectangle in the upper left-hand quarter bearing fifty small, white, five-pointed stars. The fifty stars on the flag represent the fifty states, and the thirteen stripes represent the thirteen original colonies. Use this activity to encourage your child to think of historical events that shaped your family or things that are important to them, and use those ideas to create their own personal flag.

12" × 18" piece of heavy white paper
Pencil
Acrylic or tempera paints
Ruler
Paintbrush

1. Have your child draw out a flag design using the pencil and ruler.
2. Paint the flags the desired colors.
3. They can be hung on the wall, refrigerator, or even the front door. This project can also be completed by painting a 12" × 18" piece of muslin using fabric paints.

WHAT'S HOT

▶ Before your child makes his flag, explain to him the meanings of the colors commonly used on flags. They are: blue—fairness, faithfulness, sincerity; black—grief, feeling bad; green—hope; orange—strength; purple—high rank (like a president, king, or queen); red—courage, bravery; red/purple—sacrifice; silver or white—faith, purity; and yellow or gold—honor, loyalty. Tell your child to pick his flag colors based on these meanings.

Paper-Mache Globe

Show your child a real globe and then let him create his own. Why not make two? He can decorate one to look just like a real globe, and then decorate the second any way he wants!

Round balloon	Newspaper
Paper-mache paste	Acrylic paint
Paintbrush	

1. Blow up and tie the balloon.
2. Use your choice of paper-mache pastes and paper-mache techniques as explained in Chapter 3 and have your child cover the balloon. She should apply at least three complete layers of newspaper using paper mache techniques. Allow each layer to dry before the next one is applied.
3. Once the paper-mache is dry, have your child paint the balloon to look like a real globe using blue, green, and white paint. Older kids can get more detailed if they like.

Paper Mache Masks

While we have all of the paper-mache supplies out, why not help your child make a mask? Masks have great meaning in many cultures. They can be found as art forms and for ceremonial use in cultures all over the world.

Aluminum foil	Newspaper
Paper-mache paste	Acrylic paint
Embellishment objects	Craft glue
(see ideas below)	Paintbrush

1. Tear off a piece of foil at least twice as long as your face and fold it in half. Use your child's face as a mold by gently pressing the double layer of tin foil to get a nice face mold.

2. Wad up newspaper and put it inside the curved section of the foil mold, and lay it on your work surface.

3. Use your choice of paper-mache pastes and paper-mache techniques as explained in Chapter 3 and have your child cover the foil mold with several layers of paper mache. While applying the first layer of newspaper and paste, make sure not to press on the mold too hard or it may lose its shape.

4. Once the paper mache is dry, your child can paint it and add details with embellishment objects such as yarn, fabric scraps, beads, glitter, and any other decorative item she likes.

5. While this mask is more for decorative purposes than for wearing, you can cut eye holes out before you decorate it and also punch holes on either side to add ribbon or elastic to fit around your child's head.

ASK YOUR GUIDE

How can I make a mask using plaster?

▶ Masks can easily be made using plaster strips like those used for making casts. These can be purchased at medical-supply stores or even some craft stores. Be aware that younger kids may get scared by this method, as the masks are made by molding the plaster to the face. To learn more about this mask-making option and others, visit this page on my About.com site: http://about.com/familycrafts/masks.

Get Linked

As I said before, crafts are a great way to teach kids without them even knowing they are learning, and with the ideas shared on these pages on my About.com site, they can learn even more.

PICTURES OF CHAPTER 8 CRAFTS

Visit the URL below to see colored photos of all of the craft projects shared in this chapter. You can also share photos or crafts you've completed.

http://about.com/familycrafts/chapter8

EDUCATIONAL CRAFTS

Find a variety of projects that are not only fun and creative, they also teach lessons!

http://about.com/familycrafts/educational

Chapter 9

Crafts and the Great Outdoors

Camping and Picnic Crafts

Whether you are planning a camping trip or a picnic, or you just wish you were, you are sure to find something here to spark your family's creativity.

Glow-Bug Necklace

Have your child make this easy craft while you're waiting to leave for a camping trip or on the way to your destination. After dark, he can activate the glow stick with your help and add some fun colors around the campfire.

Glow stick	Cording or yarn
Chenille stem	Wiggle eyes
Old scissors or wire cutters (for cutting chenille stems)	

ELSEWHERE ON THE WEB

▶ Camping is a popular choice for families when it comes to vacations. There are options to fit all tastes and all pocketbooks. It doesn't matter if you have a huge motor home with all of the comforts of home or if you prefer roughing it in a tent, you are sure to find something at the About.com Camping site to interest you: http://camping.about.com.

1. The glow sticks you use can be any color or size, as long as they have a loop on top you can thread the cord through.
2. Have your child cut a piece of cording to hang around his neck like a long necklace.
3. Thread the cording through the hole on the top of the glow stick and tie the ends together to make the necklace.
4. Let your child glue on the wiggle eyes toward either end of the glow stick.
5. He can then create his own unique bug by using the chenille stems to create wing shapes, antennae, legs, or anything else he wants. The chenille stems can be twisted around the glow stick to be held in place. If you wish, you can secure them with a few strategically placed drops of glue.
6. Be careful about placing chenille stems around the center of the glow stick, as you will need to bend it to activate the glowing chemicals.

Pretend Binoculars

Your child can make a pretend pair of binoculars using toilet-tissue rolls. These are fun for her to take along on a day-long hike or overnight camping trip so she can hunt for pretend lions, tigers, and bears!

2" × 6" piece of lightweight cardboard
2 cardboard toilet-tissue rolls
Paint
Craft glue

1. Have your child paint both of the toilet-tissue rolls and the piece of lightweight cardboard. Let the paint dry.
2. Show your child how to place a line of glue down both long ends of the 2" × 6" piece of cardboard.

3. Next, have her lay the toilet-tissue rolls down on the glue. Let the glue dry.
4. She now has her very own pair of pretend binoculars! If your child would like to take this craft a step further, she can add some embellishments, such as beads, feathers, or sequins.

Activity Travel Tray

You and your child can easily transform an old cookie sheet into a fun activity tray that can be brought along for camping trips.

Large, metal cookie sheet (make sure magnets will stick to it)
Black chalkboard contact paper
White memo-board contact paper
6" × 9" envelope
Magnetic strips
Dry-erase markers
Small piece of cloth
Chalk
Magnetic letters, numbers, etc.

1. Help your child cover one side of the cookie sheet with the chalkboard contact paper.
2. Cover the other side of the cookie sheet with the white, memo-board contact paper.
3. Have your child decorate the envelope with the markers or whatever else he likes.
4. Cut four 1" pieces from the magnetic strip and stick or glue them onto each corner of the front of the envelope.
5. Place the dry-erase markers, small piece of cloth (a piece cut from an old washcloth works perfectly), and chalk in the envelope.

6. The envelope holding your supplies can be stored by sticking it to the cookie sheet along with any magnets you choose.

7. This activity tray should provide hours of fun play! Your child can use the dry erase markers on the white side of the cookie sheet, and the chalk on the black side. He can draw pictures or play games such as tic-tac-toe or hangman. Once he's done, use the cloth to wipe the surface clean. It's also a nice surface to play with magnetic poetry, letters, numbers, etc.

Beach Crafts

Kids love the beach! The excitement leading up to any trip to the beach is almost unbearable, and if your kids are anything like mine, you can't come home from a visit to the beach without at least one bucket or bag full of sandy treasures. The following are a few crafts you can enjoy before, during, and after your trip to the beach.

Personalized Beach Towel

Fancy beach towels are very expensive, but everyone wants one. Follow these directions, and every member of your family can transform a plain, less-expensive towel into a one-of-a-kind, colorful creation.

> Large, white towel
> Contact paper
> Simply Spray fabric paint (www.simplyspray.com)
> Scissors

1. Wash each towel to remove all of the sizing.
2. Lay the towels flat on a well-covered work surface.
3. Use the contact paper to write personalized messages, names, or initials on the towel. You can also make abstract designs or large pictures. Draw out your letters or shapes on the right

Can I make my own fabric spray paint?

▶ Yes, you can, and it is fairly simple! Find a clean spray bottle (you will not be able to use this for anything but painting). Pour a few inches of water into the bottle. Using plain fabric paint, squirt a little at a time into the water, stirring or shaking well, until you get the desired color. You can now spray this on fabric!

side of the contact paper. Cut out your design, remove the paper backing, and stick it onto the desired location on your towel.

4. Follow the directions for the fabric paint and color the towel using one or more colors. Dry the towel according to the fabric paint's directions.

Sand Castings

While at the beach, you can make this sand casting to instantly transform your beach findings into a work of art! If you want to try this craft and you are not going to a beach, simply get some sand from a nearby sandbox or local store and pour it into a large bowl or deep tray.

Plaster of Paris
Beach findings
Large paper clip or piece of wire
Clean, empty coffee container
Paint stir stick or other disposable utensil

1. Find a spot at the beach where the sand can be left undisturbed for at least 1 hour.

2. Have your child make a shallow (1" or less) bowl-like hole in the sand to hold the plaster of Paris. You may need to add a little bit of water so the sand sticks together.

3. She can now press her treasures into the sand in the hole, nicest side toward the sand. She can either make an impression and then remove the item, or she can leave it to become part of the finished craft.

4. Mix up a batch of plaster of Paris in the coffee can following the manufacturer's directions.

ELSEWHERE ON THE WEB

▶ Many families will spend hours on the beach building sandcastles, but did you know there is such a thing as a professional sand sculptor? I could not believe the wonderful pieces of art that can be created using just sand and water. For inspiration, take a little time to visit Sandcastle Central (www.sandcastle central.com) before your next trip to the beach.

5. Carefully pour the plaster into the hole. You may want to let your child slowly spoon it into the hole.
6. To make a hanger for the sand casting, have your child stick the paper clip into the top side (determine this before you pour the plaster of Paris) of the exposed plaster of Paris after it has started to firm up a little bit. You can also make a loop out of wire and stick half of it into the plaster.
7. Once the plaster of Paris has dried, let her dig out the casting, brush off the sand, and gaze at this lovely decoration!

Another fun idea for this activity is to have your child make a shallow handprint or footprint in the sand and pour in your plaster of Paris.

Beach Magnets

Once you get home from your trip to the beach you can easily transform your found treasures into fun magnets. Let your child decide if he wants to leave them with a natural look or jazz them up with paint, glitter, ribbon, and other embellishments. He can also create simple designs such as butterflies and angels!

Beach findings (shells, sea glass, etc.)
Strong magnet backings (small, round ones work best)
Craft glue
Embellishment items (optional)

1. Have your child wash and dry all of his beach findings.
2. Show your child how to glue the magnet onto the side he wants to be the back of the magnet. Let the glue dry completely before you hang it on the refrigerator, locker, or other metal surface.

3. For a little variety, have him experiment with gluing a few shells together and embellishing them to look like angels, butterflies, and more.

Flowers

There are lots of great crafts you can make using real flowers. You can also make creative fake flowers using a variety of craft supplies. So, no matter what time of year it is, you can make fun flower crafts using these directions.

Flower Pounding

Do you believe you can transfer the color from flowers and even leaves onto fabric by beating them with a hammer? The kids especially will enjoy this creative activity, as long as they have plenty of parental supervision!

Variety of fresh flowers and leaves
White, cotton fabric (muslin works well)
Wax paper
Hammer

1. Locate a hard surface, like a sidewalk or cement floor, to work on. Cover your work surface with wax paper.
2. Have your child arrange the flowers and/or leaves onto the wax paper in whatever design she wants them to appear on the fabric. She can also just lay out one flower or leaf at a time.
3. Carefully lay the fabric over the flowers and/or leaves.
4. Show your child how she can gently pound on the fabric over the flowers and/or leaves and see the colors bleed through onto the fabric. Be careful that neither the fabric nor the flowers move!

WHAT'S HOT

▶ Many people want to know how to make crafts using candy, and with flowers this can be easy! One of the easier ways is to create simple paper flowers and glue a wrapped candy into the center. One of the more popular candy crafts are rosebuds made from Hershey Kisses. Of course, you can also make flowers using stickers. There are many possibilities, and you can find these and more on this page on my About. com site: http://about.com/familycrafts/flower.

5. Let your child continue to pound the flowers and leaves until she gets the desired results.
6. Use the fabric to make pillows, frame it to make pictures, make several to use in a quilt, or even appliqué it onto a shirt or other fabric item.

I have been told that this fabric is machine washable in cold water with mild detergent, but I opt to hand wash!

You can also use this technique to transfer color to paper. Make unique stationery, invitations, bookmarks, and much more.

Flower Pressing

If your child prefers to save her flowers rather than beating them, she can try pressing them. This process flattens them while they dry out, so you can use them in different crafts. If you have thicker flowers, the petals should be thinned out before pressing. Otherwise, the pressed flower might look more like a smashed flower!

Flowers to be pressed	Cardboard
Newspaper	Tissue paper
Heavy book or piece of plywood	Large brick or rock

1. First, have your child set out a piece of cardboard that is almost the same size as the book. Lay a piece of newspaper (about the same size as the cardboard piece) on top of that, followed by a piece of tissue paper (also about the same size as the cardboard piece).
2. Have your child carefully place his flowers on the tissue paper. Make sure none of them touch each other or hang over the side of the tissue paper.

▶ If you enjoy pressing flowers and leaves, you may want to consider building a higher-quality flower press. Use plywood and cut two pieces to the desired size of your flower press. You need to drill holes in all four corners for bolts that will be held in place by flat washers and wing nuts. To press flowers using this device, you still need to layer cardboard, newspaper, and tissue paper, but this gives you a sturdier press that can be moved.

3. Cover the flowers with another piece of tissue paper, then newspaper, and then cardboard.
4. If your child has more flowers, he can repeat this process, one on top of the other, until all of the flowers are prepared.
5. Once the stack is done, top it off with the heavy book and the brick or stone. Let it sit in a dry place until ready. This method usually takes two to four weeks.

Pressed flowers can be used in pictures, are wonderful sandwiched between two pieces of clear contact paper, and also work well as decoupage items. There are many creative possibilities!

Cardboard-Roll Flower Bouquet

Let your child create one, or an entire bouquet of these fun flowers. She can fill a vase with these flowers or fill a clay pot with marbles, clay, or floral foam and stick the skewer into it.

Cardboard tubes (from toilet tissue or paper towels)
Lightweight cardboard
Wooden skewers
Miscellaneous embellishing supplies
Craft glue
Acrylic or tempera paint
Scissors

1. Help your child cut the cardboard tubes into 3" rings. You will need a ring for every flower.
2. To make the flower petals, she should make cuts about 1½" deep about every ½" around the ring. Gently push the strips outward to look like petals.

Layers needed for pressing flowers

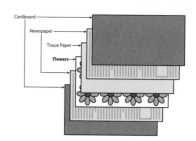

▶ Pine cones are a great ingredient for interesting crafts! You can make everything from simple ornaments to stunning tabletop decorations. Just remember that pine cones hold seeds and some may contain sap. You can avoid the mess this can cause by setting your pine cones on a cookie sheet and placing them in a 200-degree oven for about 1 hour. Find a variety of related crafts here: http://about.com/familycrafts/pinecone.

3. Let your child trace around one end of the cardboard tubes onto the lightweight cardboard. Trace and cut out enough circles so there are 2 for each flower.

4. Have your child paint the cut cardboard tube and 1 side of each circle whatever colors she wants her flowers to be. At this time, she should also paint a green wooden skewer for each flower.

5. Once dry, she should glue one end of the wooden skewer so it is sandwiched between the unpainted sides of the cardboard circles (the end should be completely hidden).

6. The round end of the cardboard-tube flower should now be glued to the circles, which will end up being the inside of the flower. Let the glue dry.

7. The inside of the flowers can now be decorated! Your child can make a sunflower by gluing real sunflower seeds into the center of a flower. She can make a fluffy center by cutting small squares of tissue paper and rolling then or pinching them, dipping them in glue, and sticking them into the center of the flower. Small pom-poms would also look cute glued into the flowers.

Crafts from Nature

While many of the crafts shared in this chapter so far can technically be referred to as nature crafts, here are my top picks when it comes to using items from nature to make original crafts.

Pine-Cone Angel

Using these directions, your family can make a collection of pine-cone angels. These make a great gift or decoration around the holidays.

Small pine cone   1" wooden-ball head

1" to 2" wide lace
Doll hair, yarn, etc.
Craft glue
Scissors

Silver chenille stem
Acrylic paint
Paintbrush

1. The pine cone will be the angel's body. Have your child paint it whatever color he likes. He can also leave it natural or brush it lightly with glue and add glitter. At this time he should also paint the wooden-ball head if he wants it a different color.
2. Once all of the paint is dry, your child can glue the wooden ball onto the pointy side of the pine cone. Depending on your pine cone, you may be able to simply slide the hole in the wooden ball onto the tip of the pine cone.
3. For the wings, I would suggest cutting two pieces of 6" lace; however, your child can use as much or as little as he likes.
4. Lay the pieces of lace on the table next to each other so the gathered edges are touching, and pinch them in the middle. Tie where you pinched with a small piece of chenille stem. Now the pinched/tied area of the lace can be glued to the back of the pine cone for the angel's wings.
5. Your child can paint a face on the angel, or it may be easier to let him draw a face on the angel using a fine-tipped marker.
6. Glue on the doll hair, yarn, or something else for the hair.
7. Add a small circle of the silver chenille stem for the halo.

Nature Sun Catcher

This is a classic craft that kids enjoy as much today, with all of the fancy gadgets and supplies available to them, as we did in our day.

Nature finds
(see suggestions)

Wax paper
Old crayons

Craft foam (optional)   Ribbon
Scissors   Cheese grater
Iron and ironing board   Hole punch
Pressing sheet or dishtowel

TOOLS YOU NEED

▶ If you prefer that your child makes sun catchers without using wax paper and a hot iron, let her try making a nature sun catcher using contact paper. The main benefit is that you don't have to seal the picture with heat. Plus, the clear sun catcher is usually more transparent than wax paper. One drawback is that it takes practice to sandwich the nature finds between two pieces of contact paper without getting wrinkles or bubbles.

1. Go for a family walk and gather small, flat items, such as leaves of different shapes and colors, grass, small flowers, and clovers.

2. Cut out two matching pieces of wax paper for each sun catcher. At this time, the wax-paper pieces should be cut into whatever shape and size your child wants the sun catcher to be.

3. Lay down one piece of wax paper on your ironing board. Have your child arrange his nature finds however he wants on top of the wax paper. Make sure the outside edge is kept clear! To add a little color, grate the crayons and let him sprinkle them onto the wax paper.

4. Lay the second piece of wax paper on top so your child's nature finds are sandwiched between the two pieces of wax paper.

5. Set the iron to medium heat. Carefully lay the pressing sheet or dishtowel over the wax paper. Press with the iron (do not slide the iron back and forth) until the two pieces of wax paper are fused together. Do not let your child near the iron!

6. While the wax-paper sun catcher cools, your child can create a frame using craft foam.

7. Finally, let your child punch a hole in the top of the sun catcher and thread a piece of ribbon through it. Tie the ends of the ribbon together to hang the sun catcher.

Nature Frame

Make lovely picture frames using twigs you gather from your backyard or a neighborhood park. Adults should use the garden shears to cut and trim the branches for the kids.

Small sticks or twigs
Acrylic paint
Paintbrush

Old frame
Craft glue
Garden shears

1. Go for a family walk and gather sticks from your backyard, a park, or the woods. I prefer straight sticks ¼" to ½" thick. They can be sticks already fallen from trees or you can use the garden shears to cut twigs.
2. Remove the back of the frame and take out the glass. Have your child paint the frame if desired. I prefer to use a color of paint that blends into the color of the twigs. Let the paint dry.
3. Your child should then generously spread glue on the frame. Let her lay the sticks on the glue, trimming them with the garden shears as necessary. She can simply lay them vertically and horizontally around the frame, or she can experiment with different arrangements.
4. Let the glue dry and reassemble the frame with a picture. If desired, embellish the frame with other objects from nature such as pebbles, leaves, or even dried flowers.

Sports

Both sports fans and athletes alike will certainly be willing to take a little time off from watching or training to make one or more of these sports-inspired crafts.

Stuffed Sports Balls

Let your child make an amusing decoration depicting his favorite sport, or a stuffed decoration depicting sporting equipment from several sports. He can make a stuffed football, baseball, soccer ball, and, even though it isn't a ball, a hockey puck!

WHAT'S HOT

▶ Picture-frame crafts are always popular. You and your child can make a variety of picture-frame crafts using many creative techniques and supplies. Whether you want to make a picture frame or two from scratch or give an old frame new life by decorating one you already have, the ideas on this page will help get your creative juices flowing: http://about.com/ familycrafts/frames.

Paper bag
Acrylic or tempera paint
Scissors

Newspaper
Craft glue or stapler

ELSEWHERE ON THE WEB

▶ After you and your child enjoy these sports-related craft projects, why not explore the Science of Sports presented by the Exploratorium, also called the Museum of Science, Art and Human Perception. This fascinating Web site explains the science of baseball, the science of surfing, the science of hockey, skateboard science, and much more. You and your child will certainly find something to interest you here: www.exploratorium. edu/sport/index.html.

1. The size of your finished stuffed sports ball will depend on the size of the paper bag you use. You can use either a small lunch sack or a large, paper grocery bag. Either way, the first step is to cut the bottom out of the bag. It will then look like a paper tube.
2. Have your child lay the bag on his work surface and draw the shape of his favorite sports item—whether it is a round ball, an oval puck, or another shape.
3. Let your child cut out his circle or oval through both layers, so he ends up with 2 cutouts.
4. Now he can use the paint to decorate the blank sides of each circle or oval to resemble a sports ball. Let the paint dry.
5. Line up the two ball pieces on top of each other, painted sides out. Glue or staple them together around the edges, leaving a 4" to 5" opening along the edge. Let the glue dry.
6. Your child can now crumple the newspaper, and even the scraps from cutting the paper bag, into loose balls and stuff them into the sports ball.
7. Once the ball is stuffed to a desired thickness, glue or staple the rest of the edge closed. If you want to be able to hang up the finished ball, add a loop of yarn or ribbon into the seam before you close it.

If you and your child would like to experiment with this craft a little bit, you can add some texture to the balls by crumpling the cut-out shapes before he paints them, and then flattening them. He can even dip them in water after he crumples them and then lay them flat to dry.

Personalized Pennant

Your kids will certainly enjoy making and displaying their own custom pennants. They can make one sporting their own name, the name of their favorite team, or just about anything else they want.

Felt fabric paint
Yard stick or dowel (approximately ½" diameter in the desired length)
Craft glue
Scissors

1. Cut out a double-pennant shape from the felt, which will be a diamond 36" long that has a point on each side and is 12" wide in the center. It may be easier to draw a pattern onto a piece of paper or newspaper and then pin it onto the felt for your child to cut.
2. Once the piece is cut out, lay it on your child's work surface. Have her drizzle glue over the entire piece.
3. Place the dowel across the 12" points of the felt and then fold it in half so you end up with a 12" × 18" triangle pennant on a stick. Trim to even up the edges if necessary.
4. Let your child decorate the pennant. She can write and draw with fabric paint or make shapes from coordinating felt. You may want to buy some self-adhesive felt letters and other shapes—they are inexpensive and very versatile!

Yard Games

Your kids will not only enjoy making this project, they will also enjoy hours of backyard fun playing these games with you. For added competition for older kids, you can write numbers on different bottles so they can play the games for points.

Fold over one edge to form pennant

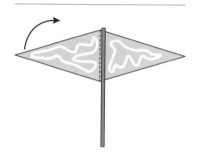

How can we create our own Olympic games?

▶ You can start out by fashioning Olympic medals, participant tags, and even trading pins. For games you can include the bowling and ring toss; create an indoor-outdoor obstacle course; make your own set of weights for a weightlifting competition; or try a tug-of-war. You can find a large variety of game and craft ideas on this page of my About.com site: http://about. com/familycrafts/olympics.

10 empty soda or water bottles (16-ounce size)
Sand or clean kitty litter
3 or more lids from margarine tubs or coffee cans
Krylon plastic spray paint
Funnel
Craft knife
Large ball (soccer ball, volleyball, or basketball)

1. Wash and dry the bottles.
2. Let your child place the funnel in the bottles, one at a time, and scoop sand into each bottle until they are almost half full. Replace the lids—you can glue them in place if you like.
3. Take the bottles to a well-ventilated area and spray paint them. Let them dry.
4. Cut out the center portion of the margarine tub or coffee can lids with a utility knife. You want to make these into rings that are about 1" thick. (Kids should not use the craft knife!)
5. Take the rings to a well-ventilated area and spray paint them. Let them dry.
6. You can now set up and play a bowling game or a ring toss game!

For bowling, set up the ten bowling pins into a triangle layout on a hard, flat surface. Make a line 6' to 8' back from the pins using masking tape. Everyone has to stand behind the line and roll a large ball toward the pins to see how many they can knock down. You can adjust the distance everyone rolls from depending on age.

For the ring toss game, set up the bottles at a variety of distances away from a drawn line. Everyone stands behind the drawn line and tosses the rings and tries to get them to land over the bottles. See who can ring the most bottles!

Get Linked

Here are some great links to my About.com site that will help you explore more outdoor-related projects. Not only will you find fun crafts featuring outdoor items and themes, you can choose crafts to complete when there are days you can't go outdoors.

PICTURES OF CHAPTER 9 CRAFTS

Visit this link to see colored photos of all of the craft projects shared in this chapter. You can also share photos or crafts you've completed.

http://about.com/familycrafts/chapter9

NATURE CRAFTS

Try a variety of free nature-related craft projects using leaves, sticks, rocks, shells, flowers, sand, and more.

http://about.com/familycrafts/nature

Chapter 10

The Art Side of Crafting

Altered Art

You're probably wondering, "What the heck is altered art?" In the simplest terms, it is a recycling craft! More precisely, it is the art of taking an ordinary household object, sometimes an unwanted object, and decorating and embellishing it to create a work of art. The focus of this art form usually comes in the items used for embellishing. The items used to embellish the objects are usually referred to as ephemera and found objects.

Technically, ephemera refers to printed matter that is usually read or used and discarded, such as ticket stubs, postcards, posters, greeting cards, etc. Some people, including me, also use this term to refer to other found objects used in altered art, such as charms, buttons, beads, and ribbon. Some of the more popular ephemera objects can be found in your own closets and junk drawers at home. These include, but are not limited to, costume jewelry, orphaned puzzle pieces, keys, and abandoned game pieces.

One of my favorite things to alter is an old, hardcover book. You can embellish every page of a book, attach a few pages together and decorate, or even glue all of the pages together and add a window to hold large objects. You can cover entire pages with decorative paper or you can use the words on the page as part of your art. You can use the cover art the book already has, enhance it, or cover it completely and design your own book cover. There are many options, which means you have more ways you can personalize your projects!

Don't limit your altered art to books; you can alter just about anything! To get you started, try picking an item from this list:

- Books
- Paper mache boxes
- Notebooks and journals
- Shoe boxes, jewelry boxes, etc.
- Frames
- CDs
- Candy or cookie tins
- Cigar boxes
- Overnight cases
- Match boxes
- Envelopes
- Knick-knacks

Of course, you can alter pretty much anything. As you go about your daily life, make it a point to look at everything you touch and think how you might be able to turn it into a work of art! You will be surprised at how many creative possibilities you will discover.

Next time you are cleaning out your junk drawer, sorting through your game closet, or strolling through a rummage sale, keep your eye open for ephemera or found objects. You can use found objects, or even parts of found objects. For example, if you come across a sweater with irresistible buttons, buy the sweater and cut off the buttons. You could also use swatches cut from the sweater, or the tags inside the sweater. Once you start thinking

ELSEWHERE ON THE WEB

▶ Before you start your own altered art project, take a little time to visit Beth Cote's Web site at www.altered book.com. She is a professional mixed-media artist and has written several how-to books sharing her skills, many of which are on my bookshelf! She is nationally recognized as the "foremost artist of altered books." Take time to read a little about her, but you should mainly drop by her site to browse through the gallery—amazing!

creatively, you will be amazed at what can be used as art materials. Here are a few ideas to get you thinking:

- Costume jewelry
- Puzzle pieces and game pieces (for example, dominoes and Scrabble tiles)
- Wire
- Shells
- Feathers
- Keys
- Nuts, bolts, washers, and other hardware
- Stickers
- Magazine pictures
- Postcards and greeting cards
- Wallpaper samples
- Charms, beads, and buttons
- Ribbon and lace
- Marbles
- Bottle caps
- Used postage stamps
- Vintage pictures, advertisements, or product information

You can use virtually anything that will fit the theme you choose and the item to be altered. The main thing to remember when it comes to altered art is that anything goes.

The only real trick is to use paint, glue, tape, and other products that are appropriate for the materials you are using. For example, you can use a glue stick to adhere a post card to a piece of paper, but you certainly wouldn't want to use a glue stick to attach wooden Scrabble tiles. You can do some experimenting when it comes to painting or attaching your ephemera to your altered item. You can try attaching ribbon to a project using an eyelet or brad. Another idea might be to create windows or pockets in your altered art projects.

While I won't share specific project directions here, because that's not what art is about, I will share a few suggestions to help get you started. Use these suggestions to jump-start your imagination and create your own objects of altered art, whether they are just to be displayed or actually used.

TOOLS YOU NEED

▶ One product you can use to make altered books is a product called Blank Board Books from C&T Publishing. What a wonderful product! These small, blank books are just waiting for you to stamp, glue, paint, draw, and embellish them. These are great for gifts, celebrations, or just for the fun of it. You can choose from several different sizes and shapes. Read more about this product here: http://about.com/familycrafts/boardbooks.

- **Book safe:** I made a book safe by gluing together all but the first few pages of an old book. I cut two small windows in the center of the book using a craft knife, and then I decorated the top page using scraps of torn paper and decoupage techniques. I opted to leave the cover the way it was. I now have this book on my bookshelf and it blends in with all of the other books—that is, until you open it! You can stash or glue treasures into the window or hide money.
- **CD photo-brag book:** Cut several pieces of cardstock to fit inside the empty CD case. Glue or tie them into the CD case to create a book. The CD case will act as the cover and back of your book. Embellish to your heart's content! Why not make it a special gift by personalizing it for Grandma, a special aunt, or best friend. Fill each page with appropriate pictures, sayings, etc.
- **Tin of quotes:** I figured out that the perfect use for a small tin—such as one that used to contain mints or candies—is to fill it with short, inspirational quotes! It was simple to cut a strip of cardstock as wide as the tin and accordion-fold it to create a little booklet that fits into the tin. Glue the end of the accordion strip into the tin and decorate the tin as desired. Add inspirational quotes all at once or fill up your book as you discover new quotes. This can also be used to write down cute things kids say, private jokes amongst friends, and so much more!

The most important thing to keep in mind when you make your own altered art projects is to make them yours. Of course, if you are giving the item as a gift, you can and should customize them for the recipient, but you should also make it personal for you. Always remember, as with any art project, there is no right or wrong way to do it.

Collage

The word "collage" comes from the French word coller which means "to glue." Collage is similar to altered art. In fact, many believe the two terms are interchangeable, and they are not wrong. Art involves a lot of interpretation, and that goes for altered art and collage. The main difference, as far as I am concerned, is that with altered art you usually start with a pre-used or three-dimensional object, and with collage you usually start with a piece of paper or flat canvas as a base.

Pablo Picasso enjoyed doing collages, but you don't have to be a famous artist to do a collage. Collage can be as basic as your child cutting pictures she likes out of a magazine and gluing them onto a piece of paper. You can use one type of medium, such as magazine pictures, or combine several together, such as tissue paper, magazine pages, tin foil, or fabric. The process can be as simple or as complex as you and your child want it to be.

Like with altered art, making a collage is not something you need step-by-step instructions for. It is more a matter of you and your child experimenting. The more you play around with making collages, the more ideas you will get. Here are some media you can play around with. You can glue, tape, or staple them onto your base.

- Greeting cards and post-cards
- Puzzle pieces
- Fancy paper
- Tin foil
- Wallpaper
- Newspaper clippings and magazine pages

WHAT'S HOT

▶ These days, crafters are incorporating collage techniques into other crafts such as scrapbooking and sewing. I experimented with collage techniques to create a graduation quilt for my daughter. I collected scraps of fabric and old T-shirts of hers. I also scanned many photos, school work, and certificates and printed them out on fabric. I sewed all of these together in a collage-type design, added some charms, buttons, and appliqués and—well, you can see the quilt here: http://about.com/familycrafts/gradquilt.

- Stickers
- Photographs
- Fabric, ribbon, and lace
- Tissue paper
- Colored cellophane
- Candy wrappers
- Leaves
- Wrapping paper
- Fancy napkins
- Playing cards

ELSEWHERE ON THE WEB

▶ While doing some research on collage, I ran across the National Gallery of Art's Web site and was particularly impressed by their kids' interactive page: www.nga.gov/kids/zone/zone .htm. I spent time playing the fun art-based games on this page, which include two online collage machines! These games offer a selection of collage items. You simply click on the items to add them to your collage, then you can resize and rearrange them. They even give you instructions for printing your collage masterpiece.

If you need something to help jump-start your creativity for a collage project, why not think of a theme to construct your collage around. You can plan out your project first or simply start gluing on pictures. Here are some ideas that may inspire you:

- **The four seasons:** Create a collage that features aspects from all four seasons or pick one season.
- **Pick a color:** Design a collage using medium of one color.
- **Pick a place:** Choose pictures featuring places you'd like to visit, such as New York or Paris, or you can choose somewhere you go often, such as the library, playground, or grocery store.
- **Self portrait:** Trace around your child and have them fill in the image using appropriate colors cut from pictures in magazines, catalogs, or colored newspapers. You can trace around just their shoulders and head or, if you have a large piece of paper or cardboard, trace their entire body.
- **Story or poem collage:** Choose a favorite short story or poem and find collage pictures depicting the verses.
- **Favorite things:** This is a fun collage idea that younger kids seem to really like. They simply browse through magazines and catalogs and find pictures of things they like and add them to their collage. When my kids were too young to write, this is how they used to make their Christmas wish lists!

- **Photo collage:** This may be one of the more obvious projects. You can make collages using photos. If you are making the collage for a birthday, you can use pictures of the person from birth on up through the years. If it is for a friend, you can include pictures of friends hanging out. Anything goes!

The art of collage is all about playing around with media, colors, and images. You and your child can't do it wrong and you can't make mistakes, you simply pick a medium and glue it down. The nice thing with collage is that if you don't like the way something looks, you can simply glue another picture on top of it. So, what are you waiting for? Go have some collage-making fun!

Painting

Children of all ages love to get creative with painting! When you hand a child a paintbrush and a blank piece of paper, she immediately becomes an artist! She will eagerly paint masterpiece after masterpiece and display them with pride.

There can be a lot more to painting than slapping a brush against a blank canvas. Let your child try painting with different household objects or use templates or stencils. You can make your own paint together, or you can experiment with painting on a variety of surfaces. There are many creative options when it comes to painting with kids!

While many people might prefer an old-fashioned paintbrush, why not try painting with one of these items:

- Cotton balls or cotton swabs
- Feathers
- Fingers
- Rags
- Yarn or string

- Toothpicks or straws
- Toothbrushes
- Spray bottle or eyedropper
- Bingo dauber
- Rollers

And, while a painting made using watercolors, acrylics, or oil paints would suit many tastes, you can make your own paint or use products you have around your house to teach your child more about painting. You can mix up one of the paint recipes shared earlier in this book, or you can add food coloring, powdered tempera paint, or even powdered drink mix to any of these products and try painting with them using a finger, paintbrushes, or any of the objects listed previously:

- Eggs
- Milk or sweetened condensed milk
- Pudding
- Shaving cream
- Water
- Glue
- Dish soap
- Yogurt
- Light corn syrup

If you want to take your child's painting experience to yet another level, try adding some texture to her paint and let her experiment with it. There are many items you have lying around your home that you can add. Try some of these and then go on a search through your house to see what else you can find:

- Sand
- Glitter
- Rock salt
- Sequins
- Spices
- Flour
- Corn starch

▶ No artist would be complete without a paint pallet. And you don't have to buy one—you can make your own. First, find a margarine container lid and about 6 plastic soda-bottle screw-on caps. You then should hot glue the caps to the inside of the lid. You can also cut out a small hole in the lid for the artist's finger to fit through. When ready to paint, simply fill each cap with a different color, and voila!

If you need a little inspiration to start a painting project, you can try some of these simple suggestions:

- **Salad-spinner painting:** If you have a salad spinner that is collecting dust, you and your kids can have a ball creating fun pictures with it. Simply have your child put a paper plate into the salad spinner, drop some paint in a variety of colors randomly onto the paper plate, put the cover tightly onto the salad spinner, and spin away!

- **Ice-cube painting:** Fill an ice-cube tray with water, stick a toothpick into each compartment to make a handle for your ice cube, and freeze. Once the ice cubes are frozen, let your child paint with the ice cube by sprinkling some dried tempera paint (or they can use mixed tempera or acrylic paint) onto paper and sliding the ice cube around on it while it melts.

- **Bread painting:** Let your child create masterpieces on pieces of bread and then eat them! You simply mix milk with a few drops of food coloring (until you get the desired color) and provide your child with a clean paintbrush. She can paint colorful designs on her piece of bread, toast it, and then eat it.

- **Marble painting:** Have your child put a piece of plain paper into a cake pan (cut the paper to fit if necessary). Put a few drops of tempera or acrylic paint on the paper. Let your child place a marble or two into the pan and tilt the pan to make the marbles roll around through the paint.

- **Resist painting:** Have your child use a white crayon to draw a picture on a white piece of paper. The picture will be invisible until your child paints over it using watercolors or watered-down tempera or acrylic paint. Let your child experiment with different colors of crayons, papers, and paints.

WHAT'S HOT

▶ Sometimes trying to think of something to paint is the hardest part of the project. Why not encourage your kids to transform a photo into an abstract work of art? This page has a great how-to: http://about.com/familycrafts/paintphoto. Make sure you follow the link to see all of the wonderful photos provided for inspiration. Keep the ideas and photos shared here in mind next time your child has trouble finding inspiration.

Painting with children can be a great way for them to experiment with mixing colors, learn about cause and affect, and stretch their imagination. You don't want to tell them how they are supposed to do it or what a finished product should look like. It is best to offer different products and opportunities and let them decide how they want to do it. The one thing you do want to do is to cover the work surface with newspaper or an old tablecloth and have your child wear a paint smock or old clothes. You may also want to keep a bucket of warm soapy water nearby, and have lots of fun!

Photography

I got a fancy digital camera as a gift, and I just can't get enough of the wonderful, artful pictures I can take with it! My current project is framed pictures of different colored lilies I have in my garden. The pictures I took of each flower were taken from about 12" away. I am going to print them all out and cut them to 10" × 10" and put them in acrylic frames. They are very colorful and will make wonderful art pieces!

The word "photography" means "to draw with light," and that is what a camera does every time it takes a picture. While we all use cameras to capture memories, you and your child can also use it to express your creativity! While the quality of your camera will affect your final picture, there are many other factors that come into play.

Of course, there is obviously much more to photography than I can cover in a few paragraphs here, but if you and your child keep these basics in mind, you will be surprised at the inspirational photographs you can take!

- **Move in close:** When you find a good subject for a picture, move closer or zoom into it to get a close-up shot, so that the thing you want to focus on fills the frame. If you have a digital camera, take what you might consider a normal shot, and then take one close up and compare them.

- **Lighting:** Good subject lighting is very important in photography. You should almost always use flash indoors, even with good lighting. Taking pictures outdoors can be tricky. Usually your best bet is to shoot a picture with the sun behind you. You will want to try to position the subject so the sun is not causing them to squint. You may even want to put the subject in a lightly shaded area and use the flash.

- **Interesting angles:** Instead of standing in front of your subject and shooting them straight on, play with some different angles. Kneel in front of the subject or shoot from off to the side; you can even get out a ladder and shoot them from above. If you're taking a straight-on shot, make sure you get down, or up, to your subject's eye level.

- **The quick click:** Shoot fast, especially when taking pictures of young children and animals. You do not want to let that perfect picture get away!

- **Watch your back:** Pay attention to what is in the background of your photo. Zoom in, reposition your subject, or switch your angle to discover the best background to enhance your subject.

- **Practice focusing:** If your camera automatically focuses, make sure you get a clear shot of your subject. If you can manually set the focus, play around with different aperture settings. Try setting your camera to a smaller f/stop number to get a smaller depth of field and more focus on your subject, and experiment with a large f/stop number to make everything in the frame come into focus.

Follow the steps above, and you and your child will be on your way to becoming better photographers. Remember, when taking

ELSEWHERE ON THE WEB

▶ If you want to learn more about photography and look at some awe-inspiring photographs, check out www.photo.net. The photos shared in the gallery are amazing, and there are some wonderful tutorials so you can learn how to use your camera more effectively. If you are looking for a camera, you're sure to find some useful information if you read through their product reviews.

pictures you're the director, so keep rearranging the scene and snapping pictures until you get that perfect shot! Once you have those perfect pictures, you can use them to create fun refrigerator magnets, print them out onto iron-on transfers, and make T-shirts, or incorporate them into many other craft projects.

Print Making

You and your child can get creative with printing, and I don't mean writing! I am referring to print making. With simple print making, you cover one item with thick paint or ink and press it onto another item to make a design.

Your child will enjoy making prints on plain paper, T-shirts, newspaper, and canvas. These techniques can even be used to decorate walls, sidewalks, and old furniture! The item used to make the print is usually something small enough to hold and/or it should have a lot of texture.

There are a variety of supplies that can be used to print patterns and pictures onto different objects. Of course, you can go out and buy an assortment of products advertised as being print supplies, however, I would suggest you start out by using your imagination and objects around your house to try your hand at making prints.

Let your child use the supplies listed here to make an assortment of creative printed projects:

- Balls
- Bubble wrap
- Bubbles
- Cardboard
- Cookie cutters
- Corks
- Fingerprints, footprints, and handprints
- Fish
- Flowers and leaves
- Fruits and vegetables
- Plastic baskets

▶ With the growing popularity of digital cameras, there is also a growing number of edit-imaging tools available. In most cases, the images from digital cameras are made better by tweaking and adjusting them using photo-editing software for your home computer. If you look at the shelves at your local computer store, you will find many options, some very expensive, so do your homework first and read more about photo-editing software here: www.imaging-resource .com/soft.htm.

- Powder puff
- Sponges
- Stamps
- Styrofoam
- Textured fabric
- Toys
- Yarn or string

You can set out an assortment of these objects for your child to play around with or just introduce one or two at a time. It may also be fun to use the same object to make prints using thick and thin paint and compare the differences. Your child can also experiment with dipping the item you are printing with into paint and dabbing the paint onto the item to get more precise results.

The fun thing about print making is that you can use just about anything to make prints just about anywhere! Use the ideas below to help get you and your child started, and then together you can think of other items you can use to make prints.

- **Bubble pictures:** Pour about ½ cup of water into a shallow dish and add about 1 tablespoon of dish soap and several drops of paint and mix well. Place one end of a drinking straw into the mixture and gently blow to make bubbles (if you do not get nice bubbles, simply add a little more soap to your mixture). Blow until the bubbles are almost over the edge of the pan. Place a piece of paper on top of the bubbles and hold it in place until several bubbles have popped and transferred their color onto the paper.
- **Cardboard printing plate:** Create your own custom stamp using a piece of cardboard and a few other supplies. Cut a base out of thick cardboard, a 3" or 4" circle or square is a great size to start with. You may want to tape or glue a handle on one side of the cardboard, such as a toilet-tissue roll. You will use the other side to create a custom printing

plate using string, noodles, and other small objects. The only trick is to make sure they are all about the same thickness.

- **Reverse prints:** Instead of printing with an object, you can print around it. For example, have your child lay a leaf on a piece of paper and use a sponge to print around the edge of the leaf and onto the paper. Lift the leaf and you will see a lovely leaf outline! Continue with several different leaf shapes and/or colors.

- **Honeycomb picture:** This is just plain fun! Have your child dip a coarse, natural sponge into yellow paint and press it on paper so it looks like a honeycomb. Let that dry and then he can dip his finger into the yellow paint and press that on the picture. Let that dry, and he can use a black marker to transform the fingerprint into a bumble bee!

Sculpting

A sculpture is a three-dimensional work of art that is usually made using clay, metal, wood, or found objects. It may be carved, modeled, constructed, or cast. A sculptor is a person who makes three-dimensional works of art. You can teach your child that he or she can easily become a sculptor.

If you and your child have ever made a sandcastle or a silly creature out of modeling clay, you have been a sculptor! Sculptors change certain materials into something original and exciting! A lump of clay can be molded into an exotic animal; a log can be carved into an expressive person; shiny metal can be twisted into fascinating structures; or, my favorite, a pile of junk can be transformed into something surprisingly new and fresh!

Sculptures are made for many purposes and can be found in many places. Some sculptures are modeled after people, such as a statue of a past president or a bust of a family member; others are more symbolic monuments such as religious figurines or even a tombstone or roadside marker! All of this aside, however, sculpture is a way for the sculptor to express his or her creativity.

You can explain to your child that sculpture has been used to express creativity for thousands of years, and encourage him to try his hand at it. Offer him some materials he can use to make a sculpture, such as:

- Clay
- Wood or metal
- Junk (trash or recyclables)
- Wire
- Rocks or sand
- Plaster
- Wax
- Popsicle sticks
- Chenille stems
- Pom-poms
- Balloons
- Butter or chocolate
- Shells

To get them started on a sculpture, have your child pick a theme, such as animals, people, or places, or he can simply plan his sculpture as he goes. When sculpting, your child can also be encouraged to explore different ways of joining pieces of his sculpture together if needed; besides just glue, he can use pins, tape, staples, nails, frosting, etc.

Here are some suggestions to help motivate and inspire you and your child.

- **Clay sculpture:** Start out by mixing up a batch of clay with your child. Pick a theme or a person to portray or opt for an abstract design, and get sculpting!
- **Edible sculpture:** Let your kids create interesting edible sculptures using frosting as glue to hold together crackers, cookies, marshmallows, gumdrops, and any other treats you

TOOLS YOU NEED

▶ When you are working with sculptures and other projects, sometimes you have to let your creations sit for a few days to dry. This can be an inconvenience if your counter space is limited, so why not use a portable work surface? Simply lay down some newspaper or wax paper on a cookie sheet and do all of your crafting on that. When you are done, it is simple to move the cookie sheet to a safe location.

want to include. Your child can also hold items together using pretzel sticks.

- **Paper mache:** Your child can use paper-mache techniques to make a wonderful sculpture. She can make large or small sculptures and create animals, astronauts, or even buildings. A paper-mache sculpture can also be an ongoing project because your child can add more paper mache anytime the urge strikes her.
- **Permanent sand sculpture:** You and your child can make permanent sandcastles and sculptures. In a large bucket, mix together 5 cups of play sand, one bottle of school glue, and just enough water so your sand and glue mixture is moldable. Lay down some wax paper on your work surface and use paper cups, bowls, boxes, and other containers to make sand sculptures! Let your sand sculpture air dry.
- **Mixed-media sculpture:** Choose a few different objects from the list above and challenge your child to create a unique sculpture using them all.

Get Linked

Explore more of the art side of crafting by visiting these pages on my About.com site. Beware—the projects shared can be addicting!

PICTURES OF CHAPTER 10 CRAFTS

Visit this link to see colored photos of some of the craft projects shared in this chapter. You can also share photos or crafts you've completed.

http://about.com/familycrafts/chapter10

PAINTING

Find out how you can use a variety of objects to paint with, discover recipes to make your own paint, and much more.

http://about.com/familycrafts/painting

PHOTO FUN

Learn more about photography and find several creative options for using photos in your crafting.

http://about.com/familycrafts/photo

Chapter 11

Seasons and Celebrations

Autumn

With autumn come football games, hay rides through apple orchards, Halloween, and Thanksgiving. All of these are great excuses to make crafts.

Football Portrait

Let your child explore his artistic side by drawing or painting a portrait of his favorite football player, or himself in football gear!

> 2 paper plates
> Crayons, markers, or paint
> Craft glue
> Scissors

1. Have your child draw or paint a face on the inside, center of the paper plate. He should also draw or paint a helmet shape along the side and top edges of the plate.
2. On the other paper plate, help him draw a grid to be the helmet's face mask. It should take up about ½ of the plate.
3. Let your child cut out the face mask and glue it, back side facing out, onto the bottom half of your paper-plate face. Your child now has a picture of a football player he can hang up!

Apple Magnet

Your child will enjoy making a magnet that looks like an apple, either with a worm or without!

Jar or frozen-juice can lid	Felt or craft foam
Chenille stems	Wiggle eye
Craft glue	Magnet
Scissors	

1. Let your child trace the lid onto the felt or craft foam. She can use red, yellow, or green to create different kinds of apples.
2. Have your child cut out the circle and glue it to the inside of the lid.
3. Using felt or craft foam, have her cut out one or two leaves and glue them onto the front top of the apple.
4. Have your child cut a 2" piece from a brown chenille stem. She can glue one end of this onto the back of the lid to be the apple's stem. At this time, she can also glue the magnet onto the back of the lid.
5. If she wants to make a worm, have her cut a 2" piece of chenille stem. Glue it onto the middle of the apple so it looks like a worm poking its head out of the apple. Don't forget a wiggle eye!

Lollipop Scarecrow

Dress up lollipops to give to your favorite kids, or have your child make them for a classroom treat.

Lollipop	Muslin
Yarn or raffia	Wiggle eyes
Marker	Craft glue
Scissors	

1. Cut a piece of muslin into a circle that is about 6" across. Pinking shears give the edge of the fabric a nice raggedy look.
2. Then cut a piece of yarn or raffia about 6" long. Lay the fabric circle centered over the lollipop. Pull the edges down around the lollipop and tie it in place using the yarn or raffia.
3. You now have a scarecrow face your child can decorate. He can glue on yarn or raffia for the hair, and wiggle eyes. Have him use the marker to draw a mouth and even stitch lines!
4. Using this technique, you and your child can make a variety of Halloween characters. You can also make larger versions of this craft by using a wooden spoon instead of a lollipop.

Paper-Bag Pumpkins

You and your kids will have a ton of fun making enough stuffed pumpkins to fill an entire pumpkin patch.

Large paper grocery bags	Paint
Construction paper	Chenille stems
Newspaper	Rubber band
School glue	Paintbrush

ASK YOUR GUIDE

What is the most popular holiday when it comes to making crafts?

▶ Would you believe the most popular holiday for crafters is Halloween? The most popular requests I get are for costume ideas and pumpkin-carving patterns. While you can find tons of both of these items on my Web site, you can also find crafts featuring a variety of Halloween creatures, ghoulish recipes, Halloween party games, and much more. Start out on my main Halloween page and start exploring: http://about.com/familycrafts/halloween.

1. Have your child paint the paper bag orange. Have her leave the top 2" brown.
2. While you are waiting for the paint to dry, have her cut a couple of leaf shapes out of green construction paper.
3. Once the paint on the bag is dry, your child can ball up small pieces of newspaper and stuff them into the bag until it is about ⅔ full.
4. Twist the opening of the bag together, and then seal the bag closed using the rubber band. The brown part will be the pumpkin's stem.
5. Spiral the chenille stem around a pencil and then remove it and wrap it around the pumpkin stem to look like a vine.
6. Have your child glue the leaves near the rubber band on the stem if she wants.

Your child can also make apples using this method and small lunch bags.

Ghost Pin

You and your child can make matching ghost pins to wear!

White school glue	Small wiggle eyes or black seed beads
Wax paper	Pin back

1. Lay a small piece of wax paper on your work surface.
2. Have your child draw a simple ghost shape onto the wax paper using the glue. Fill in the shape completely with glue. It may be easier to draw the ghost shape with a pencil first.
3. Let the glue set just a little bit and then add eyes using either the wiggle eyes or seed beads.

4. Once the glue is completely dry, you should be able to peel off the wax paper and glue on the pin back.

Turkey Candy or Nut Holder

These can be made to use as nut cups for your Thanksgiving dinner or simply for decoration.

Small clay pot
   (approximately 3")
Craft stick
Scissors

Craft foam
Wiggle eyes
Craft glue

1. Help your child cut a 3" × 1" oval out of brown craft foam.
2. He should glue one of the ovals to the outside of the clay pot, sticking up about 1½" over the top edge. This will be the turkey's head and neck.
3. Now have him cut several oval feather shapes out of red, yellow, and orange craft foam.
4. The feathers can be glued to the outside of the clay pot opposite the side with the head and neck. They should also extend above the edge of the pot 1½".
5. Let him use scraps of craft foam to make a beak and waddle, and glue on two wiggle eyes.
6. He can make a small name tag by cutting a square of craft foam and gluing it on top of a craft stick. Write a person's name on the craft foam and stick it into the pot of candy or nuts, or you can glue it onto the side of the turkey.

Turkey candy or nut holder with place card

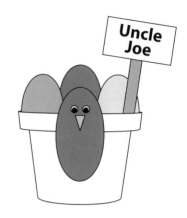

Tree of Thanks

This is a great way for your family to celebrate Thanksgiving. Have all of your friends and family members add leaves to your tree as they visit over the holidays.

Bare tree branch	Clay pot or glass jar
Pebbles	Construction paper
Pen	Ribbon, yarn, or raffia
Hole puncher	Scissors

1. Fill the clay pot with pebbles and stick the branch into them so it stands up like a tree.
2. Cut a variety of leaf shapes out of red, orange, and yellow construction paper. Use the hole punch to make a hole in each leaf.
3. Cut pieces of ribbon, about 8" long for each leaf shape you have.
4. On each leaf, a person should write something they are thankful for. The ribbon can be threaded through the hole in the leaf and tied to the tree.
5. Keep a basket full of blank leaves next to your tree so that your family or visitors can add leaves.

Winter

Not only do the winter holidays, such as Christmas and Valentine's Day, lend themselves well to making crafts for gifts and decorations, the weather often keeps us inside more, so we have more time for crafting.

Noodle Snowflakes

Use a variety of noodles to create fun snowflakes that can be hung in the window or as decorations on a Christmas tree.

TOOLS YOU NEED

▶ If you would like some printable help for your next Thanksgiving party or dinner, check out this page: http://about.com/familycrafts/thanksgivingprint. I have made a collection of matching Thanksgiving cards or invitations, favors bags and boxes, place cards, napkin rings, gift cards, and tags. They are all easy to make, they are free, and you can choose from four different, festive designs.

Noodles (see suggestions below)
Wax paper
Craft glue
Thread

1. Gather your noodles. For this craft, our favorites are elbow macaroni, wagon wheels, rotini, and bowties. Encourage your child to experiment with several different kinds of pasta.
2. Lay a piece of wax paper down on your work surface. Have your child glue together noodles to form unique snowflakes, gluing generously.
3. Let the glue dry and then carefully pull the snowflake away from the wax paper. Then use a piece of thread to hang the snowflake!

Star of David Ornament

These lovely stars can be hung on doors, windows, walls, or anything else you want to dress up!

6 craft sticks	Ribbon
Wax paper	Acrylic or tempera paint
Paintbrush	Craft glue
Scissors	

1. Have your child lay wax paper down on his work surface and paint both sides of all six craft sticks blue. While he is waiting for the paint to dry, cut a piece of ribbon about 10" long.
2. Apply a dab of glue to the ends of three painted craft sticks, and glue them together to make a triangle. Repeat with the other three craft sticks.

WHAT'S HOT

▶ Believe it or not, many people collect and display snowmen year round. You can make snowmen out of a variety of items. On my About.com Web site you can find directions for making snow people using a clay pot, light bulb, pine cone, socks, and many other items. You can also find out how to make a Texas snowman, snowman soup, and even snowman poop! Check it out here: http://about.com/family crafts/snow.

3. Turn your triangles so they face different directions; one point should be up and one should be down. Glue them together to form a six-pointed Star of David.
4. Tie the ribbon through one of the points for hanging.
5. To add a little sparkle, your child can decorate the star with glitter or sequins.

Santa Necklace

Let your kids make a fun necklace for themselves and all of their friends.

Thin ribbon or yarn	White pony bead
Red felt	2" peach or white pom-pom
White, curly chenille stem	Wiggle eyes
Glue	Scissors

1. Cut a piece of ribbon or yarn long enough to fit your child as a necklace. Have her thread the white pony bead onto the ribbon or yarn and tie the ends together.
2. Cut a fat triangle shape out of red felt. Roll the felt triangle into a cone and glue the two sides together. Trim the edges if necessary. Glue the pointy part of the hat onto the white pony bead.
3. Cut a 2" length of the white, curly chenille stem. Glue the chenille stem halfway around the peach or white pom-pom, cutting off any extra. This will be Santa's beard. Glue on the wiggle eyes just above the beard.
4. Lay the hat down so you can't see the holes in the bead. Glue Santa's face into the larger opening of the felt hat. Make sure that when the necklace is put on, the face looks straight ahead.

Tissue Angel Ornament

This little angel will look adorable on a holiday tree, hanging in a window, or tied on a gift. Your child will want to make several!

White facial tissue	Thin ribbon
Silver chenille stem	Cardboard
Aluminum foil	Black marker or paint
Glue	Scissors

1. Crumple up one piece of facial tissue into a ball shape. Put it in the center of another tissue, and fold that tissue up around the ball.
2. Tie a 10" piece of ribbon lightly around the tissue to hold the ball in place and tie it into a bow.
3. Let your child use a marker or paint to make a face on the angel just above the bow.
4. Cut a 5" piece of silver chenille stem. Form one end of the chenille stem into a circle to make the halo. Glue it to the back of the tissue head.
5. Cut another 10" piece of ribbon. Glue it into a loop shape on the back of the angel's head to use for hanging.
6. Draw angel wings onto a piece of lightweight cardboard and cut it out. Cover the cardboard wings with aluminum foil, then glue them onto the back of your angel.

New Year Party Popper

these can be party decorations or favors !

Colored tissue paper	Toilet-tissue roll
Tape	Curling ribbon
Small candies or gifts	Scissors

TOOLS YOU NEED

▶ Waiting for Christmas Day to arrive can be tough. The anticipation of Santa's visit, family gatherings, and special gifts can make each day seem like an eternity. Something we have always used to help make the wait a bit easier to handle is an advent calendar. The word "advent" originated from a Latin word meaning "arrival." Here are some advent calendars you can make to help you with the countdown to that special day: http://about.com/familycrafts/adventcal.

1. Cut a piece of tissue paper into a 12" square. Lay the square of tissue paper on your work surface and then lay the toilet-tissue roll centered on one edge of the tissue paper.
2. Tape the edge of the tissue paper onto the side of the toilet-tissue roll. Roll the toilet tissue up in the tissue paper tightly and secure the end with tape. You should have about 3" of tissue paper hanging off each end of the toilet-tissue roll.
3. Cut two pieces of curling ribbon, each one at least 12" long. Pinch the tissue paper together on one end of the toilet-tissue roll and tie it with the ribbon.
4. Now fill the toilet tissue roll with candies and/or small gifts. Pinch the tissue paper on the other end closed and tie it.
5. Use the edge of a pair of scissors to curl the ends of the ribbon and your party poppers are now ready to go!

Candy Rose Bud

Your child can make her friends and family these fun rose buds for a holiday treat.

2 Hershey's Kisses candies	Wooden skewer
Colored cellophane (pink or red works well)	Floral tape
	Cellophane tape
Craft foam or silk flower leaves (optional)	Scissors

1. Use a small piece of tape to hold the two wrapped candy Kisses together, bottom to bottom.
2. Help your child cut a piece of colored cellophane into a 6" square. Then have her place the tip of one of the kisses into

ELSEWHERE ON THE WEB

▶ You can spend hours exploring this great holiday Web site: www.holidays.net. You can look up specific holidays or simply browse through their calendars to discover a variety of holidays. For the more popular holidays, they have sections devoted to sharing history, crafts, recipes, songs, and much more. You can also send your friends and families free holiday e-greeting cards or sign up for their free newsletter.

the center of the cellophane and fold the cellophane up around both kisses. Twist the cellophane to secure.

3. Hold the twisted ends of the cellophane against the end of the wooden skewer and wrap tightly with a floral tape, winding the tape down the stick. Repeat this step if necessary.

4. If desired, your child can cut leaf shapes out of craft foam or use leaves from silk flowers and attach them to the stem using the floral tape.

Valentine's Day Butterfly

This cute butterfly can double as a card if you write a special message on the back.

Construction paper	Craft stick
Chenille stem	Marker
Glue	Scissors

1. Cut two heart shapes out of colored construction paper. They should be about 6" × 6". Trim off about 1" of the heart from the pointy side.

2. Lay your craft stick down on your work surface and glue the edges you just cut onto the center of the craft stick—these will be your butterfly's wings.

3. Flip your craft stick over and decorate as desired! You can cut smaller hearts to glue onto the heart wings or you can draw a little face with the marker. Don't forget to add antennae using chenille stems.

Spring

With spring comes nicer weather and the desire to get outside, but that doesn't mean you can't still make crafts! Use those rainy

WHAT'S HOT

▶ What child does not look forward to sharing Valentine's Day cards and treats with their school classmates? No Valentine's Day party is complete without sweet treats, heart-shaped cards, and a personalized box to collect all of the candy and cards in. You and your child can make all of these and more with the free Valentine's Day projects I offer on my About.com Web site: http://about.com/familycrafts/valentinesday.

spring days to craft inside, and bring your craft supplies out onto the porch or out in the backyard on a warm, sunny day.

Shamrock Pin

Your child will enjoy making and wearing this cute pin. Instead of putting a pin back on this craft, your child can glue a magnet on the back.

3 wooden hearts	Acrylic paint
Craft glue	Green glitter
Pin back	Paintbrush

1. Let your child paint all three wooden hearts green. Let the paint dry.
2. Glue the edges of the three hearts together to form a shamrock.
3. Have your child brush the top of the shamrock with glue and sprinkle on some green glitter.
4. Once the glue is dry, flip your shamrock over and glue the pin back onto the shamrock. Once the glue is dry, the pin can be worn!

Leprechaun's Pot of Gold

It's not easy to get your hands on a leprechaun's pot of gold, unless, of course, you make one yourself.

Plastic bowl (such as a small margarine tub)
Black and gold spray paints
Cardboard and newspaper
Scissors

1. Lay the bowl down on a piece of newspaper in a well-ventilated location and spray paint it black. It will take a few thin layers to get a nice, even coat.
2. Have your child cut a variety of circles out of cardboard and then spray paint them gold to make coins.
3. Fill your leprechaun pot with the gold you made. You can also make coins using clay.

Cereal Rainbows

Encourage your child to play with her food while making colorful rainbow pictures.

Fruit-flavored circle cereal (such as Froot Loops)
Scissors

Paper plate
Craft glue

1. Help your child cut the paper plate in half.
2. Encourage her to follow the curve of the paper plate and glue the fruit cereal on to look like a rainbow.
3. To make this craft edible, let your child use frosting to stick her fruit cereal onto the paper plate in place of glue!

Umbrella Picture

This is a fun rainy-day project that is great for all ages.

White paper
Chenille stems
Paint
Scissors

Paper baking cups
Glue
Cotton balls

TOOLS YOU NEED

▶ When St. Patrick's Day rolls around, one thing everyone needs is a leprechaun trap! Not only do they like to play pranks on people, they also have a pot of gold. Legend tells us that if we catch a leprechaun he will lead us to his pot of gold. If you would like to make your own leprechaun trap, check out the ideas and photos posted here: http://about.com/familycrafts/leprechaun.

1. Have your child cut the paper baking cups and the chenille stems in half. The paper baking cup will be the umbrella and the chenille stem will be the handle.
2. He can make as many umbrellas on his paper as he likes by gluing down a chenille stem and paper baking cup.
3. If he likes, he can mix a little blue paint with some glue and make dots of the blue glue on the paper using a toothpick, to make rain drops. He can also stretch the cotton balls a little to make clouds.

Mini Easter Basket

Not only are these useful little baskets, they are a great way to recycle!

Soda bottle (any size)	Chenille stem
Easter grass	Items to decorate (such as
Glue	ribbon, felt, beads, etc.)
Craft knife	Scissors

1. Use the craft knife to cut off the bottom of the soda bottle. This will be your basket, so make it as shallow or as deep as you like. Make sure it is an even, clean cut.
2. Make two small slits directly across from each other on the side of the basket for inserting the handle. Poke the end of the chenille stem through each slit, fold up and add some glue to secure.
3. Now you and your child can decorate it however you like. Your child can also use shapes cut from felt or craft foam, beads, sequins, or anything else she likes to decorate the basket.
4. Have your child fill the basket with Easter grass and a few treats and display!

ELSEWHERE ON THE WEB

▶ Next time you're sitting at your computer with some extra time on your hands, why not go searching for Easter eggs? I am not talking about the eggs the Easter bunny hides; this is a whole different sort of egg. These Easter eggs are surprises that the creators have hidden in their software, DVDs, etc. Find hidden jokes, games, animations, and much more! Discover hidden Easter eggs and learn more about them here: www.eeggs.com.

Easter-Egg Characters

This is a great way to recycle those little plastic Easter eggs that seem to be everywhere during Easter!

Plastic Easter eggs	Craft foam or felt
Wiggle eyes	Feathers
Pom-poms	Craft glue
Scissors	

1. Have your child grab an egg and decide what kind of character he wants to make—a bunny, a chick, or something else.
2. Encourage him to use a variety of supplies to make his characters. To make a bunny, he can glue on wiggle eyes and a pompom nose. He can cut ears out of white and pink craft foam or felt—and don't forget a pom-pom tail! For a chick, he can cut a small beak and webbed feet out of orange craft foam or felt, and add some wiggle eyes and a few feathers.
3. Help him use his imagination to create a variety of characters!

Coffee-Filter Earth

Earth Day is in April, and is the perfect time of year to make a variety of recycling crafts, along with this cool earth picture.

Coffee filter	Food coloring, blue and green
Wax paper	

1. Lay a piece of wax paper on your work surface. If you like, find a picture of the earth for reference.
2. Have your child lay the coffee filter onto the wax paper.

3. She can now draw a picture of the earth on the coffee filter by using drops of blue and green food coloring. Have her add one drop at a time and watch how the colors spread.

4. Once the entire coffee filter is colored, set it aside and let it dry. The dried earth picture can be hung up in a window or attached to the front of a Happy Earth Day card!

Summer

While summer is a season people usually prefer to spend out-doors, you can always find a little spare time to do crafts, especially when your child starts saying, "I'm bored!"

Picnic Placemat

Your entire family will be anxious to take these fun placemats on your next picnic.

Construction paper	Black paint
Black marker	Clear contact paper
Tape	Scissors

1. Have your child cut ten strips out of white construction paper (each strip should be 2" × 24"). If your paper is not long enough, tape two pieces of paper together.

2. Your child should lay these strips down side-by-side and tape the tops of each strip to the work surface.

3. Next, she should cut twelve strips of red paper (each should be 2" × 20").

4. Keeping the red pieces close together, she should weave them through the white piece of paper by going over the first piece then under the next piece and so on, alternating rows

until she has used all of the red pieces of paper. Trim edges if necessary.

5. Now, she can add a couple of ants to her picnic placemat by dipping a fingertip into black paint and making three overlapping fingerprints to form an ant's body. She can use the black marker to draw on six legs and antennae.

6. Once the paint dries, cover both sides with clear contact paper.

Mini Graduation Cap

These little graduation caps make cute decorations, fun hats for dolls, or great party favors.

Egg-carton cup	Lightweight cardboard
Yarn	Paint
Glue	Scissors

1. Have your child cut a single cup from an egg carton and a 4" square piece from the lightweight cardboard. The cardboard square and the egg cup can now be painted whatever color he desires.

2. Once completely dry, have him place the cardboard square on his work surface and put a dab of glue right in the center. Press the bottom of the egg-carton cup onto the glue. The open side should be up. When it is flipped over, it should look like a little graduation-cap board.

3. Cut yarn or ribbon about 4" to 5" long and attach it to the center of the cardboard to act as the tassel. You now have a great decoration, or even a cup to hold graduation party favors!

Weave the placemat using strips of paper

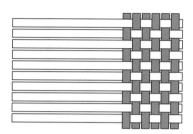

3D Fireworks Picture

Kids will enjoy making several of these fun pictures to hang up all over the house.

Dark colored paper or cardstock	Yarn
	Glitter
White school glue	Scissors

1. Lay the colored paper or cardboard on the work surface. Let your child cut several pieces of yarn in a variety of lengths, 2" to 6".
2. Squeeze some white glue into a shallow dish and mix a little water into the glue so it is the consistency of thick tomato soup.
3. Have your child dip the yarn, one piece at a time, into the glue and then lay it on the paper. Continue this with more pieces of yarn and encourage him to lay them out on the paper so they look like fireworks.
4. For a finishing touch, have him sprinkle glitter all over the yarn and then pour off the extra glitter. If the yarn dries too much, simply have him squeeze a little more glue onto the yarn.

Patriotic Treat Can

These cans make wonderful tabletop decorations if you fill them with flowers and flags, or they can be filled with treats and given as gifts.

Coffee can (or any can with a removable lid)	Cardboard
	Craft foam or construction paper
Pen or pencil	
Paint	Glue
Paintbrush	Scissors

TOOLS YOU NEED

▶ If you need to make a graduation cap larger than the miniature one shared here, you may want to check out this page: http://about.com/familycrafts/gradcap. The directions shared on this page explain how to make a graduation cap big enough to wear, or even a larger–than-life graduation cap using poster board or cardstock. These are great for kids to wear for a preschool or kindergarten graduation, or for a table centerpiece.

1. Make sure the coffee can is clean, dry, and free of any sharp edges. Have your child cover the outside of the coffee can with white craft foam or paper.
2. Cut 6 strips from red craft foam, 1½" thick and the height of the coffee can. Glue the strips vertically, around the coffee can, evenly spaced, so you end up with alternating red and white stripes.
3. Now cut a piece of cardboard into a circle about 2" wider all around than the coffee can. Cover one side of the cardboard with blue craft foam or paper and glue it under the coffee can so it looks like a red, white, and blue top hat!
4. For a finishing touch, your child can glue small, white craft-foam stars (or you can use stickers) on the blue hat brim.

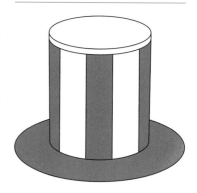

Glue the blue hat brim under the can

Shining-Star Necklace

If you and your child like to look at the stars, this is the perfect craft for you. This is also a great craft for Independence Day—simply paint the star red, white, and blue!

Clay	Paint
Clear acrylic spray	Ribbon or plastic lace
Star-shaped cookie cutter	Rolling pin
Drinking straw	Paintbrush
Scissors	

1. Help your child mix up a batch of clay shared earlier in this book, or she can use polymer or another purchased clay. Roll out the clay to about ¼" thick. Have her use the cookie cutter to cut out stars. You will want one star per necklace.
2. Show her how to use the end of the straw to poke a hole out of the star to use for hanging it. Let the clay harden by following

What can I do about the sharp edges on cans left behind by can openers?

▶ These days, many cans are available with foil-like tops that can be removed without leaving a sharp edge, or you can purchase can openers that leave no sharp edges. If you do need to use a can with sharp edges, you can try some of these solutions: hammer or pry the edges down inside the can; sand off the sharp edges; or cover the sharp edges with heavy tape.

the directions for whichever recipe you chose or product you bought.

3. Once the clay star is dry, your child can paint and decorate it as she chooses. She can use red, white, and blue paint or perhaps yellow glitter paint. Give her a few different options and let her experiment.

4. Once she is satisfied with her finished design, she can string a piece of ribbon or lace through the hole and wear it!

Watermelon Picture

This is a unique summertime craft for the entire family.

Paper plate
Acrylic paint
Paintbrush

Watermelon seeds
Craft glue

1. Your child should start by painting the top side of a paper plate red, except for about 1" along the outside edge of the plate, which should be painted green. The red will be the water-melon and the green is the rind. Let the paint dry.

2. Let him use craft glue to attach real, dried watermelon seeds onto the red part of his watermelon picture.

3. Instead of paper plates, you can use red and green construc-tion paper cut into circles.

Handprint Sun

Yet another paper-plate craft! This is a perfect craft for summer, and especially fun to make on a stormy day.

Paper plate
Paint, crayons, or markers
White school glue

Construction paper
Paintbrush
Scissors

1. Have your child paint or color the paper plate yellow. This will be the sun's face, so your child can paint either the back of the plate or the front.
2. Trace your child's hand six times onto yellow or orange paper and help him cut them out. Put a little bit of glue on the bottom edge of the palm of each handprint and press them to the back edge of the paper plate (the non-painted side).
3. The final touch is to have your child paint or draw a face on his sun.
4. You can modify this craft by experimenting with less or more hand prints, and also with different colors. Instead of a sun, he can use these same techniques to create lovely flowers.

WHAT'S HOT

▶ Sunflowers are always popular. Your child can combine the watermelon and sun crafts here and create fun sunflowers. Have her paint a paper plate brown and add handprint petals instead of sun rays. She can then glue real sunflower seeds onto the paper plate. She can also make other flowers this way if you offer her a variety of colors and objects to glue on. Try dried beans, white or colored rice, buttons, beads, or any other small items.

Get Linked

Crafts and the holidays just go together! If you're looking for more reasons to celebrate and even more projects to help you celebrate, check out these resources on my About.com site.

PICTURES OF CHAPTER 11 CRAFTS

Visit the URL below to see colored photos of all of the craft projects shared in this chapter. You can also share photos or crafts you've completed.

http://about.com/familycrafts/chapter11
↗

SPECIAL DAYS TO CELEBRATE

Find creative ideas to help you celebrate every day. Discover all of the usual and more unusual holidays for every month of the year.

http://about.com/familycrafts/specialdays
↗

Chapter 12

Making Gifts

Gifts for Her

Next time you need a special gift for one of the special ladies in your life, try making one. A homemade gift will surely please mom, grandma, and anyone else!

Blooming Magnet

Whether the gift recipient likes to garden or not, they will certainly enjoy this unique, simple gift.

Film container

Rhinestones

Cotton balls

Craft glue

Scissors

Ribbon

Magnet strip

Easy, fast-growing flower or vegetable seeds

▶ If you want to make other bath and beauty products to give as gifts along with the bath salts shared here, check out this page on my About. com Web site: http://about .com/familycrafts/bathrecipes. Any gift recipient will certainly love being able to pamper herself with a basket full of homemade bath salts, fancy soaps, sweet-smelling lotions, tasty lip gloss, and so much more.

1. A clear film container works best because then you can see the seed as it starts to grow! Start out by decorating the empty film container with ribbon, rhinestones, or anything else you desire. You can save the lid to cover the container if you are going to wrap it, but the lid should be removed as soon as the gift is unwrapped.

2. Glue a magnet strip along the side that will be the back of the film container.

3. Place two cotton balls in the film container. Sprinkle a little water onto the cotton balls and then place a few flower seeds on top. Place one more cotton ball on top of the seeds and sprinkle with a little more water.

4. Now your gift recipient can hang the magnet on the refrigerator or any other metal surface and watch it bloom! They should keep the seed moist, adding just enough water at a time to keep the cotton balls damp without making a puddle in the bottom of the film container.

5. Once the plant outgrows its magnet home, it can be transplanted into a pot or outside.

Homemade Bath Salts

These colored bath salts look wonderful if they are placed in a fancy jar; however, they are not just for decoration, they can be used!

Essential oil or perfume	Food coloring
Moisturizing oil (optional)	Epsom salts
Wax paper	

1. Place about ten drops of the essential oil of your choice into a medium-sized bowl. Add six to ten drops of food coloring and then add ten drops of the moisturizing oil. Mix well.

2. Start by adding about 1 cup of Epsom salts and mix well. You can add more Epsom salts if you like to get the desired effect or to have enough to fill a specific bottle or jar.

3. Spread the mixture out on a sheet of wax paper to dry for a couple of hours and then put it in the bottle or jar.

4. While the salts can be used right away, the perfume or essential oil will blend better with the salt and produce a stronger smell if they are allowed to set in the jar for a few weeks.

Handprint Wall Hanging

Sentimental gifts like this one are always a hit with female relatives, especially mothers and grandmothers!

Heavy paper plate (not Styrofoam)	Yarn
	Acrylic or tempera paint
Dark marker	Ribbon
Duct tape	Glue
Paintbrush	

1. Start out by letting your child paint the paper plate using whatever colors she likes. Let it dry.

2. Use a thick marker to write your child's name, age, and the date along the top and side edges of the plate.

3. Make a bow using the ribbon and have her glue it on the bottom edge of the plate.

4. Let her pick a color that contrasts with the painted plate. Paint her palm with that color and have her press her handprint onto the center of the plate with her palm closest to the ribbon. Let the paint dry.

5. If you want to hang the plate, use duct tape to attach a small yarn loop onto the back of the plate.

Gifts for Him

You can make fun gifts for all of the favorite guys in your life. Use your creativity along with these ideas.

Tool-Bench Organizer

My husband insists that I save every single empty coffee can for him, and then they disappear into the garage and workshop never to be seen again. I'm sure there are many more dads and grandpas like this out there, so this would be a perfect gift for any special guy.

Coffee can or any can with a lid
Magazines and catalogs
Decoupage medium or diluted glue
Scissors

1. Make sure any cans used are clean and dry. Have your child page through magazines and catalogs and cut or tear out pictures of tools.
3. Have her glue the pictures onto the can, covering the entire can.
4. Seal the pictures onto the can using a few thin layers of decoupage medium or diluted glue.

Personalized Neckties

When you are talking about gifts for him, you cannot forget about one of the most common gifts given to guys: neckties! Here is a new twist on this classic gift.

Paper-backed,   Fabric
    fusible webbing   T-shirt

Fabric markers and/or paint   Pen or pencil
Iron and ironing board   Scissors

1. Draw a tie shape onto the paper side of the fusible webbing. Trim around the tie pattern, staying about 1" outside of the line.
2. Let your child go through scraps of fabric and find a design he thinks is suitable for the recipient. Using the directions that came with your fusible webbing, iron it to the piece of fabric. Let cool.
3. Now cut out the tie on the lines you drew previously. Remove the paper backing and iron the fusible web-backed tie onto the T-shirt, near the neckline, where a traditional tie would be worn.
4. Your child can now personalize the tie and even the T-shirt by writing a special message for the gift recipient.

Golf-Ball Dog

They say a dog is a man's best friend, so why not make this special dog your guy can display on a shelf or even used as a paperweight! If the guy you are making this gift for doesn't like golf, you can use small Styrofoam balls that are painted to resemble the balls from his favorite sport, such as basketballs, baseballs, or soccer balls!

7 golf balls   Craft foam
Pom-poms   Wiggle eyes
Ribbon   Craft glue or hot glue gun
Scissors

1. Glue four of the golf balls together to form a square, and then glue two golf balls together. Let these all dry.

ELSEWHERE ON THE WEB

▶ Next time you are trying to find fun gifts for anyone in your life, visit the Find Gifts Web site at www.findgift.com. This site not only helps you find unique gifts, it also helps to connect you to online stores where these gifts are sold. Try out their gift wizard to be taken to a selection of gifts that meet the criteria you set. It is not only a useful service, but very interesting to browse through the wizard-picked gifts.

2. Lay the grouping of four balls on your work surface and then glue the set of two golf balls on top of them. The four golf balls are the dog's legs, and the two golf balls are the body.

3. Glue the final golf ball on top of one of the body balls. Set aside. While you are waiting for the glue to dry, cut ears and a tail out of craft foam.

4. To finish the dog, the ears, tails, and wiggle eyes should be glued on along with a pom-pom for a nose. As a finishing touch, glue a piece of ribbon around the dog's neck to look like a collar.

Gifts for Kids

These fun gifts can be enjoyed by all ages, but are especially appealing to the kids. Plus, they can be modified and personalized for both boys and girls!

Bean-Bag Toy

You and your child can make personalized bean-bag toys for everyone you know using a sock and a few other supplies. This toy is not for young kids who like to put things in their mouth!

Sock (any color or size)	Dried beans or rice
Yarn	Felt
Scrap fabric	Buttons
Wiggle eyes	Chenille stems
Pom-poms	Fabric or craft glue
Scissors	

1. Have your child fill the sock about ¾ full of beans or rice. She can then use a piece of yarn and tie the sock closed about 1" above the rice, leaving a little slack. You can also use glue to secure the yarn. Cut off any extra sock.

2. Have her divide the filled sock almost in half. You will want the toe section of the sock to be a little smaller, as this will be the bean-bag toy's head. Tie a piece of yarn tightly around the sock where it is divided, so you make two distinct sections.

3. Have your child decide what kind of creature she would like to make, such as a sitting cat or a puppy that is lying on its belly. You can make animals, people, or even make up your own creature!

4. You can now use felt to cut out arms, legs, and ears if desired. Glue these into place. Encourage your child to decorate the bean bag using a variety of items, such as buttons for the belly and eyes. She can use yarn for hair or a mouth, and don't forget about wiggle eyes and beads.

Personalized Paper Dolls

Use a picture of the gift recipient to make this fun gift idea. You can also make a few dolls using pictures of the child's friends!

Picture of child (see details below)
Lightweight cardboard
Clear contact paper
Hook and loop tape
Felt and/or scrap fabric
Buttons, ribbon, and other embellishing items
Double-sided adhesive
Craft glue
Scissors

1. To create the paper doll, you need to start out with a large picture of the child's entire body. Standing with their arms out away from their body is ideal. You can print out the picture on

TOOLS YOU NEED

▸ When I was a young girl, I loved making my own paper dolls. The main items I used for this were magazines, catalogs, and photo albums. My paper dolls were pictures of people cut out of magazines and catalogs. The photo album was my doll's house, complete with furnishings, clothes, and belongings cut from magazines and catalogs. This sounds simple, but was one of my favorite toys! If you prefer, you can print out paper dolls: http://about.com/familycrafts/paperdolls.

your home computer or get a real photograph. A full 8" × 10" would be the smallest size I would use.

2. Once you have the picture of the child, trim around the picture, about 1" outside of the outline of the child.

3. Use the double-sided adhesive to stick the picture onto the cardboard. Now trim closely around the child's outline, making sure you cut through the picture and the cardboard.

4. Cut two pieces of clear contact paper and cover both sides of the cutout. Trim to the child's outline. This will protect the paper doll.

5. Cut two pieces of hook and loop tape, about a ½" square. Glue the hook side of the tape to the chest of the doll and the other hook piece of tape just below the waist line of the doll.

6. You can now make some clothing for the doll using felt or fabric embellished with buttons, ribbons, and other items. To make clothes, you can trace around the doll onto the fabric or felt and cut out. For some fabrics you may need to add a piece of the loop tape onto the back for the doll to be able to wear it.

When giving this as a gift to a child, why not include a care package full of fabric, felt, hook and loop tape, and embellishing objects so they can make an entire wardrobe for their personalized paper doll!

Friendship Bracelets

These fun bracelets are easy enough to make that you will not only want to make them for your favorite kids, but also for yourself and everyone else you know. The colored bead you braid into the bracelet has a special meaning, so choose carefully for each recipient and make sure you let them know the meaning of the colors.

ELSEWHERE ON THE WEB

▶ If you like the bracelet crafts here, why not make several more? There is a wide variety of patterns for friendship bracelets, and if you search the Internet you will see what I mean! However, if you would rather spend your time making a variety of fun friendship bracelets instead of wasting your time searching for them, check out this page: http://about.com/parenting teens/jewelry. Denise has a nice collection of patterns and project ideas!

Here are the colors you can choose from and what each color can symbolize:

- **Red:** Energy, excitement, strength
- **Pink:** Love, friendship, compassion
- **Brown:** Comfort, reliability, the love of outdoors
- **Orange:** Energy, enthusiasm, and warmth
- **Yellow:** Joy, imagination, and optimism
- **Green:** Prosperity, healing, and growth
- **Blue:** Peace, happiness, and loyalty
- **Purple:** Calming, wisdom, and spirituality
- **White:** Protection, cleanliness, and innocence

Start out by picking the color of bead you want to work with. You can put more than one bead on a bracelet if you like; however, I prefer to only use one color per bracelet. If I want to present someone with multiple beads, I simply make them a few different bracelets.

Twine or hemp	E beads
Masking tape	Scissors

1. Cut the twine or hemp into three pieces 30" long.
2. Line up the ends of the three pieces of twine or hemp and tie an overhand knot, leaving about 3" on the end. Tape that end to your work surface and then start braiding the long ends of the three pieces of twine or hemp together.
3. Braid together your pieces of twine for about 3", and then slide the desired colored bead onto the middle piece of twine or hemp. Braid the piece together for about another 3" and then tie another overhand knot to secure.

4. Trim the ends of the twine or hemp so they are even, leaving about 3" of extra twine or hemp. The recipient can use the extra ends to tie the bracelet around their wrist.

Gifts for Teacher

These teacher gifts can be presented at the beginning of the school year, as a holiday gift, or as an end-of-school present.

Teacher's Survival Kit

This is a creative gift that is fast and easy to throw together, and sure to be a hit with any teacher. You can use as many or few of the survival kit contents as you want.

Survival-kit contents (see list below)	Small paper mache box
Paper	Acrylic paint
Printer or pen	Ribbon
Paintbrush	Craft glue
	Scissors

1. Have your child paint the outside of the paper mache box however she wants. Set aside to dry.
2. Gather together the survival-kit contents below (usually just 1of each item per kit). Write or use your computer and printer to make a small piece of paper, small enough to fit on the cover of the box, listing the ingredients from below and what each ingredient signifies.
3. Trim the page to fit and attach it to the lid of the box using small dabs of glue spaced evenly around the edges of the paper. Glue pieces of ribbon around the paper to frame it.
4. Put these survival-kit contents into the box and give to a special teacher.

What is a craft survival kit?

▶ While many of us may have created survival kits for our homes or cars to use in case of an emergency, a craft survival kit is totally different. A craft survival kit is a creative gag gift meant to not only show someone how much you care about them, but also to put a smile on their face. You can make up a survival kit for anyone in any occupation or for any occasion. Discover more here: http://about.com/familycrafts/survivalkits.

Choose one or all of these survival kit ingredients, or you can think of your own:

- **Aspirin:** When all else fails, take two and have a time out.
- **Band-Aid:** For when things get a little rough.
- **Crayon:** To color every day bright and cheery.
- **Ear plugs:** For when the noise gets too overwhelming.
- **Life-Saver candy:** Because you are a life saver to many children.
- **Marbles:** To replace those you might lose from time to time.
- **Mounds candy bar:** For the mounds of knowledge you share.
- **Paper clip:** For when you need help holding things together.
- **Peanuts:** To remind you to be a little nutty sometimes.
- **Puzzle piece:** Because you are a big piece of every child's life.
- **Rubber band:** To remind you to be flexible.
- **Starburst candy:** To give you a burst of energy when you need it.

Personalized Book Bag

Any teacher would appreciate receiving and proudly use this personalized canvas book bag!

Plain canvas bag (available at most craft stores)
Fabric paint
Fabric markers (optional)
Paintbrush

WHAT'S HOT

▶ It seems no matter what time of year it is, someone is requesting ideas for gifts to make for their teachers. I suppose there are plenty of reasons to give gifts to the people who are such important influences on our children! No matter what time of year it is, you are sure to be able to find something to make in this collection of craft ideas: http://about.com/familycrafts/teachergifts.

1. Lay the canvas bag flat on its side on your work surface. You may want to cover the work surface with newspaper before you start.
2. Paint one of your child's hands with fabric paint (whatever color he wants) and have him gently press into the center of the bag. If he leaves his fingers together, this flower will look more like a tulip; if he spreads his fingers widely, it will look like a flower with petals once he paints a small circle in the center.
3. Help your child make a row of flowers using different colors, centered across the bag. How many flowers he'll be able to make will depend on the size of his hand and if he keeps his fingers together or apart.
4. Once the flowers are complete, your child can use green fabric paint and give his flowers stems, leaves, and centers if they are needed. Let him add any other details he likes. Let dry completely.
5. Once the handprint flowers are dry, flip the bag over and lay it flat on the work surface. On this side of the bag, let your child use fabric paint or a fabric marker to write "Teachers help children grow."

Colorful Hall Passes

These handy hall passes can be hung on a door knob, cabinet door, or coat hook. Your child can make one general "Hall Pass" or several special passes that say "Office," "Library," "Nurse," "Bathroom," and "Lunch." I bet you and your child can think of more!

Craft-foam doorknob hangers
Craft foam or sticker alphabet letters
Craft foam or sticker shapes
Ribbon
Pony beads
Dimensional paint

1. Simply have your child label the foam door hanger with one of the terms above, or she can make up her own. She can write out the words using alphabet stickers, craft foam letters, or even dimensional paint. If she uses craft-foam letters or stickers, she can trace around them with the dimensional paint to add more texture.

2. Your child can also decorate the pass with stickers or fun shapes made from craft foam. As a finishing touch, have her cut a piece of ribbon about 10" long and thread one end through the hole in the doorknob hanger.

3. Now, have her hold both ends of the ribbon together and slide a few pony beads onto them. Tie the ribbon ends together and then also tie a knot above the beads to hold them in place. Your child can add a couple of more beaded ribbons to the hall pass if she likes, or decorate it any other way she pleases.

4. Let your child present these as a gift to the teacher early in the school year, and, not only will the teacher enjoy them, the students will too.

Gifts for Your Pet

When making gifts for all of the special people in your life, don't forget about your furry friends! You'd be surprised to learn how many crafts you can make for your pets, including the following.

Dinnertime Set

Your dog or cat can eat in style with a matching bowl and mat.

2 heavy bowls (the size will depend on the size of your pet)
Clear contact paper
Large pieces of construction paper (approximately 12" × 22")
Newspaper

Acrylic paints
Clear acrylic sealer
Paintbrush
Glue
Scissors

ELSEWHERE ON THE WEB

▶ You can try your hand at making pet treats to give along with these fun craft ideas. The Recipe Goldmine Web site has a large selection of recipes on this page: www.recipegoldmine.com/pets/pets.html. Not only do they have several recipes for cats and dogs, they also have recipes to make special treats for birds and horses. They even have a recipe for food to feed to a baby bird who has fallen from its nest!

1. Make sure the bowls are clean and dry. On the side of one bowl, let your child paint "Sparky's Food" (or whatever the pet's name is). He can also use a paint marker. On the other bowl, he should paint "Sparky's Water."
2. Let him decorate the plain areas of the bowl with little paw prints made by dipping a fingertip in paint and pressing a larger circle onto the desired area and then add 4 more smaller circles above the larger one using just a slight touch of the finger. Once dry, the sides of the bowl should be sprayed with a few light layers of the clear acrylic spray to seal.
3. To make a place mat, let your child write his pet's name in larger letters on a piece of construction paper. He can also make paw prints with his fingers, or even use real photos of his pet, stickers, and anything else he likes. He can also use a special fabric instead of paper. Once he has the paper decorated, cover both sides with clear contact paper.

Custom Collar

Dressing up your pet seems to be growing in popularity, and the prices of these fashion statements are sometimes outrageous! If you would like to add a little sparkle to your pet's wardrobe, make these simple personalized collars.

Plain, nylon collar
Dimensional paint

Items to embellish (rhinestones, jingle bells, fancy buttons, charms, etc.)
Monofilament
Gem-Tac glue
Scissors

1. Simply let your child embellish the collar how she chooses. She can start out by writing the pet's name using the dimensional paint if she likes.
2. Once any paint is dry, she can decorate the collar by gluing on rhinestones, jingle bells, buttons, charms, beads, or anything else she likes.
3. To secure jingle bells, buttons, charms, beads, or other heavier items, have her thread a small piece of monofilament through the hole and tie it tightly around the collar, then secure with a small dab of glue. Older children can also use an upholstery needle to sew the heavier items onto the collar.

Fishing for Pets

This pet toy is fun for both the pet and the pet owner. Try it with small dogs, cats, birds, and other pets. Just remember to put this toy up when you are not playing with your pet to avoid them chewing it up or hurting themselves.

½" dowel (any length)   ¼" to ½" ribbon
2" Pom-poms   Craft or hot glue
Scissors

1. Have your child cut a piece of ribbon as long as your dowel. He can tie one end of the ribbon onto the end of the dowel, securing it with a little glue.

A custom collar with embellishments tied on

2. Tie a pom-pom, very tightly, to the other end of the ribbon.
3. Now you can fish for your pet! Your pet will have fun chasing the pom-pom around the room. For a little variety you can tie an appropriate pet toy to the end of the ribbon.

Wrapping Your Gifts

You simply cannot give someone a fabulous homemade gift using ordinary, store-bought wrapping paper. Create your own custom wrapping paper, gift bags, or even fancy boxes. So, next time you are giving a special gift, forgo the expensive store-bought wrap and try one of these:

- Reuse color pages from newspapers or even find a special news story to share, wrap the gift using that page, and highlight sections of the story you want to point out. You can also highlight words that appear on the newspaper that remind you of the gift's recipient.
- Wrap small packages using a page or two from a calendar. You can use a page from a specific month or the artwork.
- Cut a trap door into a 2-liter soda bottle that has been washed and dried. Insert the gift along with shredded paper or tissue paper and glue or tape the trap door shut. You can also put some glitter, sequins, or confetti in the bottle!
- How about wrapping a gift using wallpaper? These come in larger pieces, fancy designs, and they are pretty strong!
- If you know someone who likes traveling, why not wrap a gift for them using a map.
- Paper grocery bags, cut apart and used inside-out, make great wrapping paper.
- Colorful magazine pictures can be used for small gifts.
- A small gift can be nestled in a little box made by taping two inverted egg-carton cups together.

- Small, paper lunch bags can be decorated using stickers, sequins, rhinestones, etc.
- I think any grandparent would be thrilled to get a gift wrapped in copies of their grandkid's school work!
- Old greeting cards can be folded into small boxes.
- Sew around three sides of two pieces of scrap fabric to create a small bag. Tie it closed with matching ribbon. You can also use a larger fabric scrap as you would wrapping paper.
- Cover or paint old shoe boxes or recycle old gift boxes.

After you wrap your gifts using one of these ideas, you can embellish it. This is a great way to personalize it to suit the personality of the gift recipient, to go along with the theme of the gift, or simply to dress up the package.

- Color or draw pictures.
- Decorate with stickers.
- Try making prints on the paper using rubber stamps, sponges, potatoes, hands, feet, and just about anything else!
- Tie it with ribbon, lace, rick-rack, or other fabric trim.
- Add a rustic flair by tying the package using twine or raffia.
- Tie on pine cones, tree sprigs, or other items from nature.
- Cinnamon sticks tied onto the gift not only look fancy, they smell wonderful!
- Make prints with cookie cutters and then tie the cutter onto the package.
- Decorate by gluing wrapped candies, such as mints or candy Kisses, dotted all over the package.

Pretty much all of these ideas are interchangeable, so be creative and experiment with what you have on hand.

WHAT'S HOT

▶ Card making is a very popular craft. It is easy to use many creative techniques and supplies to make a variety of homemade cards and invitations for all of your friends and family members. Besides inspirational ideas, on my About.com site you can find free printable cards, gift tags, and even quotes, poems, and sayings to use in your cards. Check out all of the ideas I have posted here: http://about.com/familycrafts/cards.

Get Linked

You can always find an excuse to make gifts. After you try the projects in this book, check out more projects online.

PICTURES OF CHAPTER 12 CRAFTS

Visit the URL below to see colored photos of all of the craft projects shared in this chapter. You can also share photos or crafts you've completed.

http://about.com/familycrafts/chapter12

GIFTS TO MAKE

For even more homemade gift ideas, check out this assortment of projects.

http://about.com/familycrafts/giftstomake

Chapter 13

Pick a Theme

Animals, Bugs, and Creatures

What child isn't fascinated by anything that creeps or crawls? You can spend some quality time with your child making your own creeping, crawling creatures!

Egg-Carton Animals

Use these basic directions to make a variety of animals, birds, bugs, and other creatures.

Egg carton	Acrylic or tempera paint
Construction paper or craft foam	Wiggle eyes
Feathers	Chenille stems
Paintbrush	Glue
	Scissors

Two egg carton cups glued together

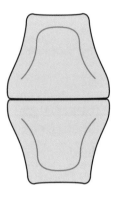

1. For each creature your child will make, cut a two-cup section from an egg carton, leaving the cups attached. Bend the egg carton cups toward each other so they are rim-to-rim (this will make an oval shape). Glue the rims together and let dry.
2. Trim off the rough edges around the section you glued so you have a nice oval, which will now serve as your animal's body. Your child can now paint her egg-carton oval whatever color she likes. Let dry.
3. Let your child use construction paper, craft foam, wiggle eyes, feathers, and any other craft supplies she likes to transform her egg carton into a cute animal. She can add craft-foam feet and beak and glue on wiggle eyes and a few feathers to make a bird. Use craft foam to make ears and a chenille stem to make a tail, and you have the beginnings of a cute kitten or playful puppy. Or how about making a sweet bumble bee with chenille stem antennae and craft-foam wings! The possibilities are endless.

Animal-Ears Headband

Your child can pretend he is an animal when he makes and wears these cool headbands. He can make many different animals and be something new every day! If you want his headbands to last a little longer, he can make them using craft foam instead of construction paper.

Construction paper
Crayons or markers
Stapler or tape
Scissors

1. Cut a strip of construction paper about 2" wide and long enough to wrap around your child's forehead. Make sure you

make it 1" to 2" longer so you can overlap the ends to be stapled or taped together.

2. Fold another piece of construction paper in half and cut out a set of ears. For a cat you will want pointy ears, for a dog, larger, floppy ears. Your child can make everything from elephant ears to bug antennae!

3. Put the bottom edge of each ear up against the inside of the strip of paper and staple or tape them in place. Your child can now color his headband if he likes. You can then fit it around his head and staple or tape the ends together to fit!

Handprint Bugs

Your child can make a variety of insects and spiders using these directions. Bugs can be hung from the ceiling on a string or piece of thread or taped to the wall to look like they are crawling.

Toilet-tissue roll	Construction paper
Wiggle eyes	Pen or pencil
Paint	Stapler and staples
Craft glue	Scissors

1. Have your child staple both ends of the toilet-tissue roll closed. If you prefer, she can tape or glue the ends closed instead.

2. Let her paint the toilet tissue roll black, or whatever color she wants her bug to be, as this will be the bug's body.

3. While the paint is drying, trace both of your child's hands onto construction paper. Let her cut out the handprints, cutting off the thumbs so there will be 4 fingers if your child wants to make a spider. If she wants to make an insect, she should cut off the thumb and a finger on each hand tracing.

TOOLS YOU NEED

ELSEWHERE ON THE WEB

▶ If you want help in figuring out what sort of bug to make, take a peek at this page at the Enchanted Learning Web site: www.zoomschool.com/subjects/insects/printouts.shtml. This educational site not only has listings of dozens of different bugs, it also has great, printable activity sheets featuring each of the different bugs. If you would rather investigate different spiders, click on the Arachnids link near the top of this page.

Handprint spider

4. Your child can glue each hand to the back of the bug's body so she has either three or four legs for each side of the body. Curl the bug's legs under a little bit to give them some shape.

5. Your child can now glue on wiggle eyes and also use scraps of construction paper to make a mouth, teeth or fangs, and any other details she wants.

Circus-Themed Projects

Everyone loves a circus, but if you don't have the opportunity to go to the circus, your family can at least enjoy making their own.

Clown Hat

Your child will have a ball dressing up like a clown with this fun hat.

Large piece of cardstock or poster board	¼" elastic
Crayons, markers, or paint	Pom-pom
Scissors	Stapler or tape

1. Cut a large triangle shape out of cardstock or poster board, making sure the bottom edge of the triangle shape can fit around your child's head. Have him decorate it using crayons, markers or paint.

2. Once decorated, roll the paper triangle into a cone, fit the bottom edge around your child's head, and staple or tape the sides together. Staple or tape both ends of a piece of elastic onto the bottom edge of the hat so it fits under the chin.

3. For a finishing touch, have her glue a pom-pom to the point of the hat.

Fingerprint Balloon Picture

Kids both young and old will enjoy this fun, yet simple, art project.

Paper
Yarn
Shallow container

Tempera paint
Markers
Scissors

1. Lay the piece of paper down on the work surface. Pour the paint into a shallow dish, and have your child dip a finger in the paint and make fingerprints to represent balloons. Let him make as many or as few balloons as he likes in a variety of colors.
2. Once the paint dries, have him cut short pieces of yarn and glue them onto the fingerprint balloons. If desired, your child can use markers to draw a circus picture around the balloons.

Cotton-Candy Craft

No trip to the circus is complete without getting some sweet, sticky cotton candy. This craft may not be sweet and sticky, but it sure looks like the real thing.

Paper-towel roll
Pink and/or blue cotton balls
Craft glue

White paper
Stapler
Scissors

1. Instruct your child to cover the paper-towel roll with white paper. Glue well to secure.
2. Now have her fluff up several cotton balls by gently pulling on them. Then generously cover half of the paper-towel roll with glue, starting at one end and adding glue all around to the

WHAT'S HOT

▶ Would you believe that you can make a variety of pictures and craft projects using mainly your fingerprints? Take a few minutes and check out these projects: http://about.com/familycrafts/fingerprint. You can make everything from adorable fingerprint frogs to apples on an autumn tree. The nice thing is that everyone can make these fun projects, and you always have the main supplies needed with you!

middle. Have your child fill her roll by sticking on the fluffed-up cotton balls so it looks like cotton candy!

3. For a finishing touch, pinch the open end of the paper-towel roll together and have your child staple it closed so it looks a little more like a cone shape.

Fairy-Related Crafts

The magical appeal of fairies knows no age boundaries; the notion of these creatures enchants both young and old! Now you and your family can try to capture a little bit of the mystical charm of fairies by making one of these fun crafts.

Fairy Wings

While these are a great addition to a fairy costume, I'm sure your child will love to wear them all of the time.

6" of 14- or 16-gauge wire
Pair of pantyhose, any color
Permanent markers or dimensional paint
Rhinestones, glitter, etc.
1" elastic or ribbon
Duct tape
Needle and thread
Glue
Scissors

1. Twist the ends of the wire together and form it into a figure 8, making sure both sides are even and the twisted ends are in the center. Twist the center of the figure 8 a few times to secure. Wrap duct tape around the center a few times to secure more and also to cover any pointy ends.

▶ If you are going to make your child a pair of wings so they can dress up like a fairy, don't forget a few other important items every fairy needs. First of all, every fairy needs a fancy nature crown made from flowers, leaves, chenille stems, and ribbons. Also, no fairy should be caught without their fairy dust; why not carry it along in a fancy necklace. To make these fairy accessories and more, give this page a visit: http://about.com/familycrafts/fairy.

2. Cut the legs off of the pantyhose. Slide one of the pantyhose legs onto each loop of your figure eight. Pull them tight in the center and tie the ends together into a bow.

3. You can now shape the wings so they look more like a butterflies', or however you like. To get the pantyhose to follow the shape the wire outlines, you can attach the pantyhose to the wire using a needle and thread.

4. Now you can decorate the wings! Add some color using permanent markers or dimensional paint and then embellish with rhinestones, glitter, or anything else you desire.

5. Cut two pieces of elastic about 30" long. Tie them around the center of the wings (where you used the duct tape) so they form two big loops. You should adjust the size of these loops so they slide over the wing wearer's shoulders like a backpack and the wings fit snuggly.

Hand and Foot Fairy

Talk about a handmade craft project! Your kids will have fun making this fancy fairy using a footprint, a couple of handprints, and a few other supplies.

Colored cardstock or craft foam
Crayons or markers
Glue
Scissors

1. Have your child choose the color she wants her fairy wings to be, and trace each of her hands on that color of paper or craft foam.

2. Next, let her choose what color she wants her fairy's body to be. Trace one of her feet on a piece of paper or craft foam of that color.

ELSEWHERE ON THE WEB

▸ Can you believe in this high-tech day and age that even the tooth fairy has a Web site? Grab your kids and visit her online at www .toothfairy.org. As you might expect, she has information posted about proper techniques for brushing and flossing, plus a FAQ about baby teeth and other educational information. She also has some fun elements like tooth-fairy tales and an interactive feature showing where the tooth fairy comes from.

***How can I use these fairies
if I don't have any plants?***

▶ You can forgo the wooden
skewer and use the plain
fairy. Try gluing a heavy
magnet to her back, adding
a string to hang her, or even
gluing her directly to the surface you want to decorate. If
you want to leave the skewer
in place, you can poke it into
a vase or jar filled with marbles, pebbles, or even beans.

3. Finally, draw a circle for the fairy's head, about 3" across, on colored paper or craft foam.
4. Have your child cut out the hand and foot prints along with the circle.
5. To assemble the fairy, glue the circle head on to the heel side of the footprint. Glue both hands on the back of the footprint to be the wings.
6. Have your child color her fairy, adding facial features and any other details she likes. To dress it up a little, she can add some glitter to the wings. You can also layer large leaves or flower petals to cover the skirt. Use yarn to make hair and any other details you can think of.

Flower-Fairy Plant Pokes

These little fairies will look beautiful flying around your houseplants or in your flower gardens.

2 wooden craft knobs, ½"	Plastic or silk flowers
3 flat, wooden ovals, 1" × ¼"	½" ribbon
Pony beads	Wooden skewers
Yarn or doll hair	Acrylic paint
Paintbrush	Glue
Scissors	

1. Paint one of the ½" knobs whatever color you want your fairy's shirt to be, and the other knob whatever color you want the fairy's face to be. Let dry. Paint the three wooden ovals whatever color you want the fairy wings to be.
2. Separate the flower from its stem. You might be able to simply pop it off, but you may have to cut it.

3. Glue the bottom of the flower (where the stem was) to the flat side of the knob you painted to be the shirt.

4. Cut a piece of ribbon about 10" long. Glue the center of this ribbon onto the shirt knob, opposite the flower. This will serve as the fairy's arms, so you may want the ribbon color to match the shirt color.

5. Dab some glue onto the flat side of the head knob and glue it on top of the shirt knob, covering the ribbon.

6. Glue one of the wooden ovals centered horizontally onto the back of the shirt bead. Glue one end of the other two wooden ovals at a 45-degree angle onto the center of the first oval. When looked at from the front, these should look like the fairy's wings.

7. Place some glue on one end of the wooden skewer and poke it into the center of the flower. The other end of this skewer is what you will poke into the ground. Let the glue dry.

8. Make your fairy some hands by slipping a pony bead onto each ribbon end and tying. Cut off any extra ribbon.

9. Finally, you can paint a face on your fairy and add some hair.

Medieval Crafts

If your child is enchanted by royalty, wizards, and dragons then he is bound to enjoy these craft projects.

Medieval Hats

Use these simple directions to make a variety of hats. You can make a royal crown, a jester's cap, or a wizard's hat.

Craft foam	Dimensional paint
Rhinestone	Jingle bells
Glue	Scissors

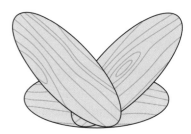

Three wooden ovals glued together to form fairy wings

1. For any of these hats (crown, jester, or wizard) start out by making a headband using craft foam. The headband should be about 2" wide and long enough to fit around your child's head with a 1" overlap.

2. To make a simple crown, cut about six triangles (about 2" wide × 4" tall) out of craft foam. Your child can match the color of their craft-foam headband or choose a contrasting color. Glue the bottom edge of each triangle along the top edge of the headband—you may have to use more or less depending on the length of the headband. Let your child decorate his crown using rhinestones and dimensional paint. Glitter paint would also be fun.

3. To make a jester's cap, you also need about six triangles, except these triangles will be about 2" wide × 10" tall. When making a jester cap, I think it's fun to make each triangle a different, bright color. Once again, glue the bottom edge of each triangle along the top edge of the headband—you may have to use more or less depending on the length of the headband. These triangles will flop over the outside of the headband. To add a finishing touch, glue a jingle bell onto the tip of each triangle.

4. To make a wizard's hat, simply cut out 1 large triangle about 6" wide × 10" tall. Traditional colors for a wizard's hat would be dark blue, dark purple, or even black, but your child can make his hat any color he likes. Glue the triangle onto what will be the front of the hat. Add yellow or white star and moon shapes to the hat using shapes cut out of craft foam or with dimensional paint.

Fire-Breathing Dragon

Kids of all ages will love making and then playing with their very own dragon.

Cardboard toilet-tissue roll   Orange tissue paper
1" pom-pom   Wiggle eyes
Paint   Paintbrush
Glue   Tape
Scissors

1. Let your child paint the cardboard tube green to be the dragon's head. She can leave it just green, or she can add details like scales, nostrils, teeth along the side, and anything else she might want.

2. While she is waiting for the paint to dry, she can cut several strips from orange tissue paper (you can use other colors, but I usually choose orange to represent the fire). She will want about twelve strips that are ½" wide × 10" long, although the length can vary a little.

3. When the paint on the tube is dry, help her tape an end of each tissue strip to one end of the tube. The tissue should be taped just inside the tube opening to hide the end. She can tape on as few or as many tissue-paper strips as she likes. This will represent the dragon's mouth and the fire.

4. Now she can make the dragon's eyes by gluing two green pom-poms side-by-side onto the center of the roll. Glue the wiggle eyes onto the pom-poms facing the side of the tube with the fire.

5. Once your child has completed her dragon you can show her how to make it breathe fire. Gently tuck the tissue-paper strips into the opening they are taped in and have your child blow hard on the other end of the tube. Watch how the dragon seems to breathe fire!

Build A Castle

No kingdom would be complete without a castle. You can help your child make a castle big enough to hold him, or a table-sized version for dolls and stuffed animals. The great part about making a castle is that you and your child can make it any size, shape, or color you want. All you need are glue, tape, utility knife, paint, and a bunch of recyclable items. Here are a few ideas to get you thinking:

ELSEWHERE ON THE WEB

▶ Before you start building your own castle, take a little time to check out this Web site: www.castles.org. You can browse through pictures of real castles from around the world, explore haunted castles, or view listings of castles for sale. For castle-making help, explore their kids' section, which features a section teaching us about the different parts of a castle, including coloring-book pages to print out.

- **Large cardboard boxes:** These can be attached together and embellished to form a castle big enough for kids to crawl through.
- **Cereal boxes:** These make great walls for small, tabletop castles.
- **Paper-towel, toilet-tissue, and wrapping-paper rolls:** These are great for making turrets. Top each one with a Styrofoam cup for an added touch.
- **Small cardboard boxes (for example, macaroni and cheese):** These can also be used as walls, or they can be transformed into furniture for your castle.
- **Wrapping-paper rolls or toothpicks:** Depending on the size of your castle, use one of these items as a flag pole. Make a flag out of paper and tape it to the pole.
- **Sponges:** Why not spongepaint the cardboard to look like stone.
- **Yarn:** Use yarn to create a drawstring bridge from a flap cut out of the cardboard.
- **Fabric:** Use scrap fabric to make royal curtains, rugs, or to cover furniture. You can also use a large piece of blue fabric to create a moat around your castle.
- **Magazines, catalogs, and greeting cards:** It's fun to use these things to cut out pictures to be hung on your castle walls. You can even frame them with craft sticks!

Musical Crafts

At one time or another, many of us or our children have grabbed an old oatmeal container and started banging on it like a drum, or used a toilet-tissue roll as a kazoo. Why not expand on these home-made instruments and try creating your family marching band.

Noise Shaker

This fun rattle is a perfect addition to any marching band.

Paper plate
Rice, unpopped popcorn, or dried beans
Strips of tissue paper, crepe paper, or fabric (optional)
Paint
Paintbrush
Stapler or tape
Scissors

1. Paint the bottom side of the paper plate. Let it dry.
2. Fold the paper plate in half so the side you painted is on the outside.
3. Place a handful of rice, popcorn, or beans inside the folded paper plate and then staple or tape the side shut.
4. Cut or tear thin strips of tissue paper, crepe paper, or fabric and staple them around the already stapled edge of the noise shaker.
5. To play this instrument, your child simply shakes it. She can also lightly tap one side like she would a tambourine.

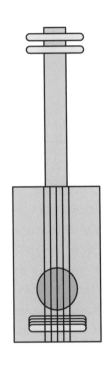

Shoe-Box Guitar

Show your kids how they can transform an old shoe box into a fun guitar.

Shoe box	4 to 6 rubber bands
6 craft sticks	Yard stick or ruler
Glue	Paint
Paintbrush	Scissors

1. Have your child paint the shoe box and the lid whatever color he wants his guitar to be. He can also paint the yard stick or ruler. Cut a circle in the center of the box lid and then replace it on the box.
2. Have your child glue four craft sticks, one on top of the other, between the hole and the short side of the box. These sticks should be parallel to the short side of the shoe box. He can then glue two of the craft sticks onto the flat side of the yard stick or ruler near one end. These sticks should be perpendicular to the yard stick. Leave about 1" of space between the two sticks; feel free to cut the sticks in half if they're too long for you. Let the glue dry.
3. Stretch four to six rubber bands around the box so they lay over the craft sticks and also over the hole. Glue the end of the yard stick without the craft sticks onto the backside of the guitar (side without the hole). It's okay for the stick to cover the rubber bands. You can also use heavy tape for this. To play this fancy guitar, your child simply plucks or strums the rubber bands.

Hand Bells

Not only are these a great addition to any homemade band, they'd also be nice to play during the holidays!

Paper-towel roll   Yarn
12 jingle bells   Upholstery needle
Paint   Paintbrush
Scissors

1. Let your child paint her paper-towel roll if desired.
2. Cut a piece of yarn about 10" long and thread it onto the upholstery needle. Poke the needle through the cardboard roll, about ½" from one of the ends, going in on one side and coming out directly across from it on the other side. Leave a 3" tail of yarn where the needle went in. Now thread four jingle bells onto the needle, pulling them down the length of the yarn.
3. Grab the yarn tail you left and also the end you strung the bells on, and tie them into a knot, pulling tightly so the bells are snug against the cardboard roll.
4. Cut another piece of yarn, thread it onto the needle, and add another string of jingle bells like you did the first. This one should be about 1" down from the first.
5. Repeat the above steps again so you end up with three rows of jingle bells. Now shake away and enjoy!

Pirate Crafts

If it's high-seas adventures your family is yearning for, why not transform your family-room sofa into a pirate ship and make these fun crafts with all your mateys?

Polly's Treasure Chest

Your child can decorate her own treasure chest, complete with a parrot watching over its contents!

Small, wooden chest	1" wooden craft knob
¾" wooden craft knob	Chenille stem
Wiggle eyes	Craft feathers
Rhinestones	Acrylic paint
Craft glue	Paintbrush

1. Let your child paint the treasure chest brown, or whatever other color she desires. Paint both craft knobs green, or any other parrot color. Let the paint dry completely.
2. Glue the ¾" painted knob, hole-side-down, on top of the 1" knob.
3. Cut a piece of chenille stem approximately 2" long. Fold it in half and then fold it in half again. Glue it on for the parrot's beak. Glue on two wiggle eyes, and then glue on feathers to resemble the tail feathers and wings.
4. Open the treasure chest and glue the parrot onto the edge. If the lid will not sit at a 90-degree angle, you can glue it to the side of the parrot's body.
5. Glue rhinestones onto the treasure chest and top it off by filling the treasure chest with chocolate coins!

Pirate's Eye Patch

Your child can pretend to be a pirate with this easy-to-make eye patch. For an added touch, tie a bandana around his head and give him a spyglass (empty paper-towel roll).

▶ You can make a large selection of crafts using wooden bits and pieces. While craft sticks are widely available, how about all of the other fancy shapes? One of my favorite Web sites for craft supplies is S & S Worldwide. You can browse through a ton of craft supplies and even kits online, including several pages of wood shapes. Explore their Web site here: www.ssww.com.

Black craft foam	Black elastic
Pen or pencil	Hole puncher
Scissors	

1. Use the pen or pencil to draw an oval on the black craft foam that is big enough to cover one of your child's eyes. Cut out the oval and use the hole punch to make a hole on each side of the oval.
2. Cut a piece of black elastic long enough to fit around your child's head. Tie one end of the elastic to one hole in the eye patch. Have your child hold the patch up to his eye, and then you can wrap the elastic around his head and tie the other end to the other hole in the eye patch.
3. Trim off any extra elastic and your child can wear his eye patch. He can also decorate it if he likes.

Pirate Flag

Every pirate needs a flag! Flags are sometimes used by pirates as a way to identify each other, so everyone should design their own unique flag that represents them.

| Craft foam or felt | Dimensional paint |
| Craft glue | Scissors |

1. Start out by cutting pennant shapes out of the craft foam.
2. Let your child decorate the flag using a variety of shapes cut from craft foam. You can help her cut out a skull and cross-bones, treasure chest, parrot, coins, a ship, and any other pirate-related shapes you can think of.
3. She can use dimensional paint to write her name or a special message on her flag.

Get Linked

If you're still looking for that perfect craft to fit a specific theme, check out these pages on my About.com site. You may just find that perfect craft for a birthday party or other occasion.

PICTURES OF CHAPTER 13 CRAFTS

Visit the URL below to see colored photos of all of the craft projects shared in this chapter. You can also share photos or crafts you've completed.

http://about.com/familycrafts/chapter13
↗

CRAFT PROJECTS BY THEME

Make crafts related to everything from animals to transportation; also included is a listing of free coloring-book pages.

http://about.com/familycrafts/bytheme
↗

Chapter 14

Pick a Product

Buttons

I love buttons! If I started counting all of the buttons I've collected, it would take me days and days to finish. You can find buttons in a large selection of colors and styles, and the shapes available are too numerous to count. Buttons can be used in a variety of crafts. Get started with the ideas shared here and let them motivate you.

Polka Dot Pots

You can make these decorative pots in a variety of colors and sizes and use them to gather small items on a dresser, to hold cooking utensils, or to organize your office supplies.

Terra-cotta clay pot	Buttons
Paint	Paintbrush
Craft glue	

1. Start out by having your child paint the entire clay pot. You don't need a saucer for this craft; however, if you have one, consider painting it and using it upside down as a lid for the pot.
2. Once the paint dries, he can glue buttons all over the pot so they look like polka dots. Let the glue dry.
3. When the glue is dry, he can fill the pot with whatever he likes and display it with pride.

Button Jewelry

Your child can make unique bracelets, necklaces, and even rings to give as gifts or to wear themselves. With the variety of buttons available you can make dozens, and no two will be alike. If you have some extra buttons lying around but no elastic thread or stretch cord, you can use dental floss! While it's not stretchy, it is very strong.

Buttons	E beads (optional)
Elastic thread or stretch cord	Scissors

1. Start out by measuring the elastic thread or stretch cord by holding it around your or your child's wrist, neck, or finger. Cut a piece about 6" longer than your measurement.
2. String on a bead or button and tie to secure, about 3" from one end.
3. Your child can now start stringing buttons and beads onto the thread or cord. She can string the buttons through both holes to make the button lay flat, alternating with coordinating beads if desired.
4. Once your child has the desired number of buttons and beads on her piece of jewelry, tie the two ends together. You can remove the first anchor bead you tied on if you like.

▶ If you would like to decorate your buttons either before you use them as craft supplies or after, you can use a product you probably have lying around your house right now. It's nail polish! Nail polish is a great craft tool, especially when it comes to adding color and texture to small items such as buttons. It sticks well to plastic, is virtually permanent, and has a nice shine once dry!

Button Bouquet

You and your child will have a grand time making an entire bouquet of these charming flowers. These look lovely when made with vintage buttons and also with the brightly colored buttons widely available these days.

Buttons   Colored cardstock
16- or 18-gauge floral wire   Scissors
Wire cutter

1. Have your child cut a variety of small flower shapes out of colored cardstock. The size of the flowers will depend on the size of the button, which will serve as the center of the flower. Cut a piece of floral wire about 20" long, or the length you want your flower's stem to be.

2. Now it is time to assemble the flowers! First, have your child poke one end of the wire through the center of a cardstock flower. Make sure he only pokes the wire through about 2".

3. Next, that same wire end can be poked through one of the holes on a button. Push the button down until it sits right up next to the cardstock flower. Now that same wire end should be bent and poked through the other hole in the button and also back through the flower. Twist the wire end around the wire to secure.

4. You and your child can experiment with using a variety of flower shapes and buttons. If you prefer, you can forgo the flower petals and let your child string two or three colorful buttons on a wire to form the flower and center.

What is the difference between a pipe cleaner and a chenille stem?

▶ These days these two terms are pretty much interchangeable. They were originally designed to clean pipes, but have found a home in many craft cupboards over the years. Today's pipe cleaners, or chenille stems, come in a variety of shapes and styles and are made especially for crafting, however, you may be able to find white, cotton pipe cleaners at a smoke shop.

Chenille Stems

Not only are there many craft projects that incorporate chenille stems into their designs, but there are several craft projects you can do using chenille stems as the main component! You can give your child a pile of colorful chenille stems, and you'll be amazed at the designs she comes up with. For inspiration, she can try some of these craft projects using chenille stems.

Peek-a-Boo Mouse Bookmark

These adorable bookmarks peeking from between the pages of a favorite book may encourage your kids to read more. They also make fun pocket sitters—if the long chenille stem is placed in your child's pocket, it looks like his little critter is peeking out.

2 gray chenille stems	1 (1") gray pom-pom
2 (10mm) pink pom-poms	1 (10mm) gray pom-pom
1 (5mm) black pom-pom	Wiggle eyes
Old scissors or wire cutters	Craft glue

1. Cut two 1½" pieces of gray chenille stem. Gently bend them both into a circle to form the mouse's ears and glue them into place on the 1" gray pom-pom. Glue a 5mm pink pom-pom into the center of each circle.
2. Glue the wiggle eyes onto the pom-pom just below the ears. Glue the 10mm gray pom-pom onto the face, centered just below the eyes. Glue the 5mm black pom-pom onto the ½" pom-pom for the mouse's nose.
3. Fold the other gray chenille stem in half. Hold the two ends together and put a generous dab of glue on them. Push the glued ends into the bottom of the mouse's head where the neck would be.

4. Cut a 6" piece off of the gray chenille stem. Fold each end in to meet in the center. Bend it into a "V" shape. Place a few drops of glue onto the bottom of one side of the "V", near the point. Glue the "V" to the bottom of the mouse's head. The top sections of the "V" shape should be under the face to form the mouse's arms.
5. Once the glue is completely dry, bend the arms so they are pointing down.
6. Slip the chenille stem into a book or even into your pocket so only the arms and the head of the mouse are sticking out.

Lion Finger Puppet

Start out by making a lion finger puppet, and then use the same techniques to make other animals and even people. Your whole family can take turns putting on fun puppet shows.

Brown chenille stem	1" tan pom-pom
2 tan chenille stems	1½" tan pom-pom
Black pom-pom	Wiggle eyes
Old scissors or wire cutters	Craft glue

1. Cut the brown chenille stem into twelve 1" pieces. Put a dab of glue on the end of one of the brown chenille pieces. Stick it into the 1" tan pom-pom. Repeat this with the other eleven chenille-stem pieces, forming a circle around the pom-pom to be the lion's mane.
2. Glue the black pom-pom onto the center of the tan pom-pom. This will be the lion's nose. Glue the wiggle eyes on just above the nose. Cut two 1" pieces of tan chenille stem. Bend them into small "V" shapes and glue them just above the eyes to be the lion's ears.

Chenille stem bent into the V shape

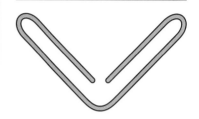

3. Put a dab of glue onto the 1½" pom-pom. Set the lower back of the head, behind the mane, onto the glue. Let the glue dry.

4. Now you can make the lion's arms and legs. Using the tan chenille stem you cut the ears off of, cut two 2" pieces and two 3" pieces. Glue the 2" chenille pieces in place to be the arms, and the 3" pieces toward the bottom of the 1½" pom-pom to be the legs. Bend the very ends of the arms and legs into a small curl.

5. Using the other tan chenille stem, wrap it around your finger to make it a spiral shape. Carefully slide it off your finger and glue it to the bottom of your lion's body, between the legs.

6. Once all of the glue is dry, you can carefully slide the spiral chenille stem onto the end of your finger and put on a puppet show! If your lion or any other creature you create is a little too heavy to stand straight, fold an extra chenille stem in half and glue it to the back of your puppet.

Chenille-Stem Flowers

Sunflowers were my inspiration for this craft. You can use these directions to make a nice collection of flowers. Display them in a vase or pot, glue them onto a notebook or journal cover, or transform them into a magnet.

Bump chenille stems
⅕" pom-pom
Chenille stems
Craft glue
Old scissors or wire cutters

1. Have your child choose two bump chenille stems in the color she wants her flower petals. Let her cut each bump chenille

stem into four pieces, making sure to cut between the bumps. She should end up with eight bump pieces.

2. Carefully bend each bump in half, and twist the two cut ends together. Your bent bumps should now look like teardrops; these will be your flower's petals.

3. Glue the rounded edge of each chenille-stem petal to a pom-pom. Start by gluing two on directly across from each other. Glue on two more directly across from each other and spaced evenly between the first two. Fill in the gaps left with the remaining four chenille petals.

4. Roll 2" to 3" of one end of the green chenille stem into a tight spiral shape. Glue the spiral to the back of the brown pom-pom to form your flower's stem.

5. Finally, cut a green, bump chenille stem in half, making sure you have 2 bumps on each piece. Fold each piece in half and pinch the ends together. Glue onto the flower's stem to look like leaves.

Clothespins

If you are lucky enough to have a bag of clothespins lying around you can start crafting right away. If you don't have them lying around, you can find the spring-type clothespin at almost any grocery or discount department store. You should be able to find one-piece wooden clothespins in any craft store, both the flat and round head varieties.

Clothespin Dolls

These little clothespin dolls are called worry or trouble dolls by some people. Guatemalan children tell their worries to similar dolls and place them under their pillows, and, according to legend, the dolls take their worries or troubles away. This is a fun craft that can be modified so even the youngest kids can make lovely dolls.

Old-fashioned, one-piece, wooden clothespins	Chenille stems
Fabric scraps	Embroidery floss
Fine-tipped permanent markers	Paint
	Yarn and/or doll hair
Paintbrush	Craft glue
	Scissors

1. The round part on the top of the clothespin will be the doll's head, and the two sides that clip onto the clothes will be the legs. When decorating the doll, make sure the legs are facing the right way (when you look at the front of your doll you should be able to see both legs).

2. Now you can make some arms for the doll. Cut a chenille stem in half and find the center. Hold the center of the chenille stem against what will be the neck of the clothespin and wrap each end around it once, pulling each arm over to the opposite side. You can fold up the tips of the chenille stem arms to act as hands.

3. Give your doll some personality by drawing a face using fine-tipped, permanent markers. Also add hair using yarn or purchased doll hair.

4. Dress your doll. It can be as easy as painting the clothespin, or you can glue on clothes made from scraps of fabric. You can also wrap your doll in embroidery floss to make clothes. To make a shirt, secure floss with a dab of glue and wrap the embroidery floss tightly around the doll, stopping at where the waist would be, again securing with a dab of glue. You can also use this same technique to make sleeves, pants, or a skirt.

5. Don't forget the finishing touches. Use paint or a marker to draw on shoes. Make jewelry using chenille stems, rhinestones, and other small embellishments.

Clothespin Critters

Once you have a clothespin doll or two, why not make some adorable clothespin animals to go along with them!

3 flat, one-piece, wooden clothespins	Small pom-poms
	Chenille stems
Wiggle eyes	Ribbon
Paint	Craft glue
Paintbrush	Scissors

1. Paint the three clothespins appropriate colors, like brown. One of them will be the animal's head and the other two will be the legs and body.
2. Start out by gluing two of the clothespins' flat sides together so the prongs line up, as they will be the critter's four legs.
3. Glue the third clothespin, flat sides together, onto the two clothespins you previously glued together; however, you will turn this one so the prongs face the opposite direction of the other prongs. These will be the critter's ears.
4. Now add the finishing touches! Glue a pom-pom onto the rounded part of the head clothespin to be the nose and glue the wiggle eyes just above it. You can also add a cute bow by the ears or under the chin. Don't forget to add a tail!

- For a puppy, make a little collar using ribbon and a pink tongue hanging out of his mouth.

Glue three clothespins together to form the animal's body and head

- To make a horse, use yarn to make a mane and long tail. You can also make a little saddle and a bridle using felt, and paint on some hooves.
- For a reindeer you can add antlers using chenille stems and perhaps a few jingle bells. A reindeer also needs hooves.
- A rabbit would need big teeth and a pom-pom tail. I bet you can think of many more!

Greeting-Card Holder

This is not only great for holding Christmas cards or birthday cards, you can also use it to hold photos. The great thing is, you can decorate it to coordinate with your room decor!

Yardstick	12 two-piece,
Paint	spring-type clothespins
Craft glue	Paintbrush

1. Let your child paint the yard stick and the clothespins whatever color he likes. Let them dry.
2. Glue the clothespins onto the yard stick, spacing them evenly, about every 3". Glue them so they are perpendicular to the yardstick, and also alternate the side the pinching part of the clothespin is on. Let the glue dry.
3. At this time, he can also paint or write a special message down the yard stick or decorate the yard stick with bows, rhinestones, buttons, or anything else he likes.

Craft Foam

Like chenille stems, I like to use craft foam in my crafting quite a bit. It is a wonderful substitute for paper and felt and is stronger and more stable than both. The nice thing about craft foam is that it is fairly inexpensive and you can find it not only in large sheets, but also a variety of precut shapes. For almost instant crafts, you can buy craft-foam visors, bookmarks, or doorknob hangers and decorate them with self-adhesive craft-foam letters, numbers, or other shapes.

Fortune Cookies

While you can't eat them, these unique cookies are so easy to make that you and your child will want to make one for everyone you know. You can make them to give or to keep, and can glue a magnet or pin back to them or add string for hanging. You can also use them to make a surprise announcement. These are also great favors for birthday parties, baby or wedding showers, anniversary parties, and many other events.

Craft foam	Paper
Pen	Hot glue gun or craft glue
Scissors	

1. Choose what color you want your cookies to be. The obvious choices are tan or a beige color, but you can make them any color. Cut out a 3" circle for each fortune cookie you want to make.
2. Before you assemble the cookie, you need to make the fortunes! Cut as many 3" × ½" (approximate) strips of paper as you have circles. Write special messages, quotes, fortunes, or other sentiments on each slip of paper.
3. Now to assemble the fortune cookies. Fold a craft-foam circle in half without creasing it. Glue the edges together to form a half circle, leaving about 1" open on each end by the fold. Let cool or dry, depending on the type of glue you use.

ELSEWHERE ON THE WEB

▶ If you want some fortune-cookie inspiration, check out this wonderful page: www .goodfortunes.com. Not only can you see several pictures of fortune cookies, and even order custom-made fortune cookies, you can browse through their collection of Cookie Quotes to find fortunes for your own cookies. They have quite a selection of quotes for a variety of holidays and celebrations and even more quote collections relating to life and love!

4. Push a fortune into one of the open ends, making sure it sticks out a little bit. Now you need to gently push the ends you did not glue together, putting a dab of glue where the two sides come together to form the fortune-cookie shape. This will be similar to a "U" shape; the folded edge will be the inside of your "U" shape and the glued edge will be the outside. Hold your cookie shape until the glue cools or dries.
5. Make several and fill a Chinese take-out box with them!

Gift-Card Purse

Give these along with gift cards, or have your child make one to carry her own gift cards, student IDs, or other cards.

Craft foam
Eyelet
Key ring, clip, or ball chain
Embellishment objects (optional)
Large needle and embroidery thread
Glue
Scissors
Pinking shears or decorative-edge scissors (optional)

1. Cut out two pieces of craft foam, approximately 3" × 5". You can cut these with the regular scissors or make fancy edges using pinking shears or other decorative scissors.
2. Hold these two pieces together, and stitch 3 of the sides together using 3 strands of embroidery thread and the needle. Leave one of the 3" sides open. Sew about ¼" from the edge.
3. Put an eyelet in one of the corners of the unsewn side of the purse. This will be used to insert the key ring, clip, or ball chain.

4. You can now personalize the purse if desired. Write the recipient's name or a special message. You can embellish with craft-foam shapes, rhinestones, etc.

Creative Mouse Pad

You and your child can make your own mouse pads to suit your individual personalities and decorating styles. These also make fun gifts.

Craft foam
Non-slip shelf liner
Permanent markers
Plain white paper (you can also use newspaper)
Embellishment objects (optional)
Craft glue
Scissors

1. Cut a piece of non-slip shelf liner the same size as the craft foam. Cover one whole side of the craft foam with a thin layer of craft glue, then lay the shelf liner on top of the glue and make sure it is smooth. Let the glue dry completely; you may want to put it under a heavy book as it dries.
2. Have your child decide what shape he wants his mouse pad to be. It can be square, round, or even in the shape of an animal! The only trick is to make sure it has a wide shape so there is plenty of room to maneuver the computer mouse.
3. Draw out your design on a plain piece of paper. Cut it out and then trace it onto your craft foam. Cut around your tracing through both the craft foam and the non-slip shelf liner.
4. Now you can use the permanent markers to decorate your mouse pad. If you made it in the shape of an animal, you can draw eyes, a nose and mouth, and any other details you like.

▶ Why not try to make your own stamps using craft foam? First, draw out your design or pattern on a piece of paper, cut it out, and trace it onto the craft foam. Using a pair of scissors or a craft knife, cut your shape/design out of the craft foam and glue it onto a bottle lid, wood block, or other object you can use as a handle. Paint your design and stamp away!

If you made an abstract or geometric shape, you can draw designs, write your initials, add an inspirational quote, etc.

5. It you want to use embellishment objects like ribbon, rhinestones, rick-rack, and so on, glue them to the outer edge so they don't get in the way of the mouse. Your mouse pad is now ready to use and enjoy!

Craft Sticks

I can't count on two hands how many times my kids have sat down and built entire villages and other projects using craft sticks. Keep a box of these inexpensive crafting supplies on hand, and you'll be prepared the next time your kids start getting the boredom bug! If you would like a little inspiration for making crafts using these fun sticks, try some of the ideas shared here and then expand from there.

Craft-Stick Vase or Pencil Holder

You can make these decorative tabletop or desk containers using either tin cans or toilet-tissue rolls. I prefer the slender look of the toilet-tissue rolls (plus, you don't have to worry about sharp edges), but if you need a sturdier container use a tin can. Of course, if you want to use this as a vase for real flowers, you need to use a tin can so you can fill it with water. But if you make your flowers using different craft supplies they will last forever in either vase.

Several craft sticks (the number needed will depend on the size of your can or tissue roll)
Toilet-tissue roll or tin can
Cardboard
Rubber bands
Craft glue

▶ Not only are craft sticks a classic craft supply, they can also be used as craft tools. Craft sticks are very handy for applying and spreading glue and paint. They can also be used for pushing bubbles out of decoupage pieces or for applying rub-on decals to just about any surface.

Acrylic paint
Paintbrush
Scissors

1. Paint the craft sticks whatever color or colors you like. Let them dry.
2. If you are using a toilet-tissue roll, cover one of the holes with a circle cut from cardboard. Trace around one of the toilet-tissue roll ends onto the cardboard, cut it out, and glue it onto the end of the toilet-tissue roll.
3. Glue the painted craft sticks around the outside of the toilet-tissue roll or tin can until it is completely covered.
4. Once you are done gluing on the craft sticks, wrap a few rubber bands around the can to hold the sticks in place until the glue dries.
5. Make several in different sizes. You can also embellish the cans with wooden shapes, buttons, sequins, or any other craft supplies you have on hand.

Elegant Candle Holder

These are lovely tabletop decorations and are fancy enough to be used at parties or even something as formal as a wedding reception!

34 crafts sticks
Wax paper
Flat embellishment items (such as stickers or paper cutouts)
Double-sided adhesive
Votive candle in holder
Craft glue
Scissors

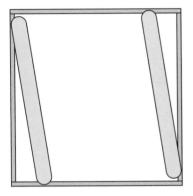

1. Cut out four pieces of wax paper into at least 8" × 8" squares. They can be bigger, but not smaller. Lay these on your work surface.
2. Squeeze some glue onto one side of four of the craft sticks. Lay these on the center of one of the pieces of wax paper to form a square. The ends should be touching, but should not overlap.
3. Repeat this with 12 more craft sticks and the wax paper pieces so you end up with 4 squares.
4. You can now add any embellishments you like. Use the double-sided adhesive to stick the items to the wax paper. If you are using stickers, you can stick the adhesive side of the sticker onto the wax paper. Keep in mind that any directional objects, such as letters and numbers, should be backwards, as they will be on the inside of the candle holder and you will only see the shadow. Make sure you use a dry adhesive so that the wax paper doesn't bubble!
5. Once any glue is dry, trim the wax paper around the craft sticks so there is no extra hanging over the edges.
6. Now lay these, design side down, onto your work surface. Glue craft sticks onto the wax paper on top of the craft sticks you glued on first, so the wax paper edges are sandwiched between two craft sticks.
7. Run a bead of glue down the edge of a craft stick on one of the squares. Stand it on your work surface and press the glue onto the craft-stick edge of one of the other squares. Repeat this with the other squares until you have all four glued together to form a square box-like candle holder. Let the glue dry.
8. To make the candle holder more stable, glue the last two craft sticks at an angle around the bottom edges.
9. Light the candle and place the candle holder over the candle surface. Watch how beautiful the light is flickering around the

shadows of the embellishment objects you attached to the wax paper.

Jewelry or Dresser Box

You child will have fun creating boxes to hold her jewelry and other treasures. She can experiment making a variety of sizes.

Crafts sticks	Wooden craft knob
Craft glue	Paint
Paintbrush	

1. If you want your box painted, it is easiest to paint each craft stick before you glue them together, especially if you want the sticks different colors.
2. Start out by making the bottom for the box. Lay twelve craft sticks evenly, side-by-side on your work surface. Spread glue on one side of another craft stick and lay it perpendicular, along the edge, on top of one of your rows of twelve. Glue another craft stick similar to the first on the other edge of the row. Repeat step 2 to make a lid for your box.
3. Now you can start building up the sides of your box. Put a dab of glue on both ends of two different craft sticks. Set each of these, glue side down, so the ends rest on the ends of the two craft sticks you glued on in the previous step. Now dab glue on the ends of two more craft sticks and lay them on top of the two you just glued on. Continue this step until your box grows to the height you want it.
4. For a nice finishing touch, glue a wooden craft knob on the center of your lid. You can also glue 4 beads to the bottom corners of the box to give it feet.

TOOLS YOU NEED

▶ Check out Ranger Industries's multi-purpose, non-stick craft sheet, which provides protection to a crafter's work surface for many craft mediums. This larger (15" × 18"), reusable, non-stick craft surface is perfect for working on scrapbooking, rubber stamping, painting, altered-art books, and more. It is heat resistant up to 400 degrees and it repels liquids. The best part is that it allows for easy clean up. You can read more about this great product here: www.rangerink.com/product _craftsheetlg.html.

Get Linked

This chapter offers a taste of what you can find online at my About. com site. To explore more, visit these pages.

PICTURES OF CHAPTER 14 CRAFTS

Visit the URL below to see colored photos of all of the craft projects shared in this chapter. You can also share photos or crafts you've completed.

http://about.com/familycrafts/chapter14

CRAFT PROJECTS BY PRODUCT

Browse through collections of crafts sorted by the products used to make the project. This does not include basic craft products such as paper, crayons, glue, etc.

http://about.com/familycrafts/byproduct

Chapter 15

After Crafting

Clean-Up Help

While crafting with your kids should always be an enjoyable experience, it does have a down side. Sometimes the supplies you use to make fabulous crafts can cause quite the mess. You shouldn't let this stop you from crafting, but you should be aware of it and even plan for it.

One of the best ways to deal with the mess some craft products leave behind is to prepare for it before you start crafting. There are things you can do to your environment and your craft products to make cleaning up easier. There are also some handy tips you can try.

You can start out by preparing your work surface. The first thing many people will grab to cover a work surface is newspaper. While this is better than using nothing, paint, markers, and other products can soak through it onto your tabletop or counter. My favorite thing to cover a work surface with is wax paper. Not only will it protect your tables and counters, the glue and paint from

▶ There are a few different tools you can use to help keep little fingers clean while trying to paint or glue small objects. The first is a pair of tweezers. These are wonderful for holding small pieces; however, manipulating these can sometimes be tricky. If this is the case, try rolling a piece of masking tape and sticking it to the back of the object. The other side of the tape can be stuck to a pencil or similar object.

your drying products will not stick to it. There is nothing more frustrating than trying to pick up a finished craft project and having the newspaper stick to the dried paint or glue.

Old, vinyl tablecloths or shower curtains also work well for protecting a work surface. These are also nice to put down on any carpet in the craft area and also to cover furniture. Not only will these protect a variety of surfaces, they are also very easy to wash with soap or water, and can even be thrown in the washing machine.

The next thing you will want to protect from stray paint, glue, markers, and other craft supplies is your child. A special arts and crafts smock is ideal, but an old, long-sleeve shirt of mom's or dad's works well, especially when worn backwards. If your child won't wear that, you can try an old T-shirt or apron. You can buy canvas aprons at most craft stores and let your child personalize it.

If your child wears an old T-shirt or apron, you can recycle old socks to protect his forearms or sleeves. Simply cut off the toe of a sock and sew or glue one of the short edges of a 2" to 3" piece of both a hook and loop tape opposite each other on top of the sock. Make sure the tape pieces are each facing the correct way, so they can be hooked together. Your child can now simply slide the sock up his arm and secure it using the hook and loop tape.

There are also a few tips you can follow to make cleaning hands and any other body parts a little easier:

1. Keep a container of baby wipes near your craft area. These are handy for quick clean ups!
2. When painting with acrylic or tempera paints, try adding 1 to 2 squirts of dish soap to the paint.
3. Keep a tub of warm, soapy water and an old dishtowel near the craft area, so that items that need to be washed don't have to be carried over carpet or other flooring.

All supplies and tools should be cleaned thoroughly after a craft session, and put away so they will be ready the next time you need them. If you keep a tub of water near your work surface, placing paintbrushes, sponges, stencils, and other items in the tub as soon as you and your child are done using them will help to ensure any paint or glue doesn't start to dry before they are washed. You can then take them to a sink or hose and wash them thoroughly with soap and water.

Before you wash any craft product down your drain, you should read the package and make sure it is safe to do so. There are some products, such as plaster of Paris, that can clog your drains and give you other headaches. Make sure you read all the package labels ahead of time so you can be prepared when clean-up time comes around.

Even when you are very careful, accidents can happen. You can run to the store and buy expensive cleaners, or use one of these household remedies for cleaning and removing the more common craft-related spills and stains:

- **Glue:** On hard surfaces, try dabbing on a little vegetable oil, peanut butter, or Avon's Skin-So-Soft. Let it sit for several minutes and then rub gently. For fabric, gently scrape or peel off what you can, then wash with warm, sudsy water. If this doesn't work, try saturating the spot with vinegar and let it sit for twenty minutes. Try scraping it again and dab it with a rag. Wash again with warm, soapy water.
- **Crayons:** On fabric, try spraying a little bit of WD-40 (a spray lubricant) onto the spot and dab clean with a rag, then wash the area with liquid dishwashing soap and water. You can also try this on walls and other hard surfaces, or try scrubbing with baking soda mixed with just enough water to make a paste. Rinse and repeat as necessary.

▶ Removing stains can be tricky. No one method will work every time, and some substances stain more easily than others. If you have a tough stain or are just looking for some general clean-up information, check out this site: www.howtocleanany thing.com. You can choose Stains from the menu and then select carpets, clothing, or hard surfaces. You can also browse through their tips and hints.

- **Acrylic or tempera paint:** Paint must be removed while it is wet. Dab, do not rub, the fabric to soak up as much paint as possible. Rinse the area with cold water and wash as usual. Do not dry unless the stain is gone. If the stain persists, lay the fabric on a white rag and dab with rubbing alcohol—the paint stain may be transferred to both rags. Walls and other hard surfaces should simply be washed with warm, soapy water.
- **Ink pens:** For either clothing or walls, try using hair spray. You can also try blotting the area with rubbing alcohol.
- **Markers:** The hardest stain to remove! On a hard or fabric surface you can rinse (wipe) with cold, soapy water until no more ink comes out. Try dabbing it with the tip of a rag or cotton ball dipped in rubbing alcohol, and rinse with cold water. Treat clothing with a laundry stain treater and wash. You may do this several times without drying; once your item is put in the dryer, the stain will be set forever. For a hard surface, you can try scrubbing gently with a liquid cleanser.

When it comes down to it, the trickiest part of cleaning up after your crafting adventures might be getting your child to help! Don't give her a choice when it comes to helping, but you can make her feel like she has some control by letting her decide what to do first. Also, it is easier to clean up if everything has a place to go. Decorate coffee cans or plastic containers to hold different supplies. This is a great way to make sure everything is put where it belongs. Finally, if you sing a song together or play some music while you clean up, your child is more likely to stay involved and interested.

Storing and Organizing Craft Supplies

No matter how many good intentions we have about keeping the craft supplies neatly stored away and organized, it sometimes seems an impossible task. Over the years, I have learned some tricks when it comes to storing craft supplies and staying organized, and I am happy to share these with you.

Right now I am fortunate enough to have my own office and crafting room, which is full of shelves and cupboards, not to mention my desk and work table. While this is ideal, it is not practical for everyone. If you do not have an entire room you can devote to crafting, start out with a corner of a room. The dining room works well, as there is already a workspace (table), but you can choose whatever room you have the space in.

Devote the entire area to your crafts. If you can put up some shelving or cupboards it will make life much easier. I recently invested in some stackable shelf and drawer units, and I love them! You can find a combination of open shelves, cubby holes, drawers and cupboards that all stack neatly together to make one large wall unit.

If you can't invest in something like these right away, you can use anything from an old dresser to cardboard boxes, shoe boxes, coffee cans, ice-cream pails, canning jars, and so on.

It is also nice to have a table devoted to crafting. You will get a lot more crafting done if you can leave unfinished projects out on your work surface, ready to go whenever there are a few spare moments. A card table is handy because it is small enough to stay out of the way, yet big enough to allow a few people to work together. It can also be folded up and put away when necessary.

As you gather supplies, sort them in a fashion that makes sense to you. In my craft room, I have all of my fabric together, sorted by color; I have all of my paint together, sorted by use; and I have all of my general craft supplies together, such as pom-poms and chenille stems, sorted by type. I prefer to store all of my different kinds of glue together in one spot, while others may prefer to keep a certain kind of glue together with the product it is used for, such

TOOLS YOU NEED

▶ Looking for a way to easily organize smaller craft items, but don't have a lot of room to spare? Buy a plastic, over-the-door shoe organizer! These are usually under $10 and provide a lot of pockets for storing craft supplies. The best part is that you can store quite a few items without taking up any counter or drawer space, plus you can easily find everything with the see-through pockets.

▶ **If you want to try a fun and unique product to decorate your craft room or area, as well as your craft supply containers, check out Wallies at www.wallies.com. These prepasted, vinyl-coated wallpaper cutouts are a wonderful way to create great-looking walls and accessories and come in a large variety of patterns. Wallies are easily applied with water and will quickly enhance and beautify any smooth, flat surface, and they are just as easy to remove.**

as fabric glue with any fabric. The key is to sort things in whatever way makes the most sense for you.

If you already have supplies but just need to organize them, take your time and go through each item one at a time. Some things, such as paint and glue, can dry up or go bad and are taking up unnecessary space. Other products you may have bought but never used, and probably never will use. Why not gather these together and donate them to a nearby daycare or nursing home?

One of my favorite things to use to store and organize my craft supplies are plastic storage bins with removable lids. They come in a variety of sizes and colors, but I prefer the clear ones so I can see from a distance what is in it. I also label each bin using masking tape and markers. While I use the large (18-gallon) bins for storing supplies, I use smaller plastic bins (1- to 3- gallon sizes) to hold the supplies for whatever projects I am currently working on; this keeps the project handy for taking it with me if I go somewhere. These bins also stack nicely in closets and other spaces and keep things dry and clean.

Another staple in my collection when it comes to organizing my craft supplies are zip-top bags. I use pretty much every different size available. They are great for sorting small items. For example, you can use the small, snack-sized bags to sort pony beads by color, and then put all of your smaller bags of pony beads into a larger, gallon-sized bag.

There are a handful of other organizing tools you can collect and try. Try one or more of these:

● **Multi-compartment boxes:** In most instances, these are made to hold small hardware items such as nuts, bolts, etc., but I use them for sorting craft supplies! My favorite use? I use one for my button collection—I can easily store buttons sorted by color, shape, etc. For an added bonus, the kids usually love helping with the sorting process!

- **Mobile toolbox:** My family thought I was crazy the year I asked for a toolbox on wheels for Christmas! There are small compartments and larger compartments, perfect for holding quite a variety of supplies and tools. Of course, you can use this to make any craft-project portable, but I use mine to store and transport all of my quilting and crafting supplies when I go away on my biyearly quilting and crafting retreat.
- **Drawer storage system:** These plastic mini-dressers are perfect for storing just about anything. They are available in many sizes, from extra wide to tiny, tabletop models. They are easily moved, and some even come on wheels. I have several of these and don't know what I would do without them!
- **Tackle box:** You can transform a fishing tackle box into a great storage box for all of your smaller craft supplies. You can find tackle boxes in a variety of shapes, sizes, and colors!
- **Milk crates:** Not only can you possibly find these for free at a school or restaurant, you can find these in most stores in a variety of fashionable colors. They can be used separately or stacked to create an entire wall shelving unit.

One more thing you should consider using for organizing and storing your supplies is a clipboard. What for? Well, on my clipboard (which I decoupaged using colorful scrapbooking paper) I keep a list of all of the supplies I have, and how many of each item. I also keep a list of supplies I need to buy the next time I go shopping, plus items I want to try. This may sound a little silly, but it really pays for me to stay organized, because my nearest craft store

ELSEWHERE ON THE WEB

▶ Being organized is always good, whether we're talking about a craft room, kitchen, or garage! Sometimes the main reason we don't get organized is that we just don't know where to start. If I were you, I would start off by visiting the Fly Lady Web site at www.flylady.net. You will find wonderful ideas and inspiration for organizing not only your household, but also your body.

What can I do with all of the craft magazines I collect?

▶ Well, what I do with pretty much every magazine I get is cut them apart! I read them and then cut out the projects and patterns that interest me. I them slide these into a plastic page protector, sometimes gluing or taping them to cardstock. I then keep these projects in binders. I now have four binders on my desk with all of the projects organized by type, instead of piles of magazines!

is almost 100 miles away, so I don't want to forget anything when I go craft-supply shopping!

Whether you use all or just a few of these ideas, you will find your craft time more pleasurable and rewarding. Not only will you know what supplies you have and where they are, you will also have more time for crafting. Hopefully, that means you will have more time to spend together creating as a family!

Saving and Displaying Arts and Crafts Projects

As a parent, one of the biggest crafting dilemmas you may face is what to do with all of the wonderful arts and crafts masterpieces your child creates. How do you display each piece so it gets the attention it deserves? What do you do with works of art that must be retired to make room for newer pieces on the refrigerator or shelf?

I think the most common way to display your child's work is to stick it on the refrigerator. While this may be the best way to display homemade magnets, it may not always be the best way to display completed arts and crafts. Since we hope that our child pours a lot of creativity into his projects, why not use a little creativity while displaying their projects.

I'm sure if you put your mind to it you could think of different, creative ways to display your child's projects, but here are some ideas to help jumpstart your brain:

- Display flat pieces in old picture frames, or take pictures of dimensional projects and frame the photos.
- String a clothesline around the room and use decorated clothespins to hang up the projects.
- Cover an entire wall with corkboard either in your child's room or in a common room, and let him hang his arts and crafts projects using colorful push pins.

- Use artwork to cover boxes, book covers, or other items you can leave out for display. You can use decoupage techniques or attach the artwork using clear packing tape.
- Hang art and dimensional craft projects in the window so they can be seen from outside.
- Laminate flat artwork or cover it with clear contact paper and use them as placemats, coasters, or table runners. You can glue a few matching pieces together on a coordinating piece of paper to make larger pieces.
- Make a personalized calendar that features an appropriate piece of art each month. This can be as simple as gluing your child's artwork over the art of an existing calendar or as fancy as taking photos of the projects and having a calendar custom made. Alternatively, you can scan your child's artwork and create your own calendar pages using a desktop publishing or graphics program. There are many ways to accomplish the results you want as explained here: http://about.com/familycrafts/calendar.
- Use scanned images or photos of your child's arts and crafts to create personalized note cards.
- Use your computer to turn your child's masterpieces into wearable art. Simply scan or take a digital photo and print the image out on iron-on transfer paper. You can not only decorate clothing, but also pillow cases, sheets, wall hangings, tablecloths, and several other household items.
- Use smaller printouts to create pin-on buttons you can wear. You don't have to have an expensive button maker, you can use clip-together buttons found at any craft store. You can also print these pictures onto shrink plastic, then trim, bake, and attach a pin back to them.
- Use images of your child's artwork as desktop patterns and even screensavers on your computer.

TOOLS YOU NEED

▶ If you are going to hang artwork and other important papers on your refrigerator, why not make your own customized magnets to go with them? You can use many creative techniques and a variety of supplies to make a selection of fun magnets using the directions on this page: http://about.com/family crafts/magnets. Not only are homemade magnets functional and decorative, they also make wonderful gifts for grandparents, teachers, and anyone else.

Now, what do you do when the shelf life for your child's arts and crafts projects have been reached? You hate to just throw them away, but on the other hand, if you keep every piece your child creates, every nook and cranny of your home, garage, and even garden shed will be full by the time your child is done with school. While some may think it is horrible to discard kid's crafts, artwork, and even school work, most kids don't care that much. Sure, they'll have their favorite pieces, but they won't insist on preserving everything. With the younger kids, making arts and crafts is more about the process to them, so some may not even seem interested in displaying their finished projects at all.

I have plastic bins full of homemade puppets, cards, ornaments, and other creative undertakings made by my children, but I have been selective enough over the years that the number of saved items is manageable. I have one 18-gallon plastic bin for each of my children that holds special artwork, school papers, craft projects, and other mementos. I usually let my children periodically help me decide what items we should keep and which ones to remove from the collection.

Flat projects can be stored in portable file boxes. You can hang a folder for each grade in the file box and let your child put her artwork in the appropriate folder. Of course, eventually you will have to weed through the folders to make more room, but you may be able to look back on a piece made three years ago a little more objectively when it comes to discarding it. Also, this way you and your child can look through the papers more easily whenever you like.

One idea I came across that I really like is the idea of scrapbooking your child's crafts. If you take pictures of your child making the craft, and even a photo of them holding the completed project, you can preserve the craft project in photos in a scrapbook. You can also write information about the craft, such as if it was made as a gift, what your child's favorite part of making it was, and so on. This way you can dispose of the project when it is time and have it saved in a scrapbook instead of taking up space in a plastic bin.

Another idea I came across that I absolutely love is videotaping your child holding each project they make. Simply have him sit with his project, and you can even interview him by asking questions such as where he made it, why he made it, for whom, and so on. I think this is a great way to capture a picture of each project and also your child's explanation of it. Once you get enough footage, you can make a mini-movie or highlight film.

Finally, don't forget to share the artwork. One way to avoid storing it is to give it away! Your child's arts and crafts projects would make a perfect gift for grandmas and grandpas, aunts and uncles, and even close neighbors. Let your child go through her saved artwork and pick out what items to give to different people. Let her put the selected projects in a box and wrap them with her own artwork!

Selling and Donating Your Crafts

When it comes to selling craft projects made by you and your child, I would think twice about it. Sitting down and doing crafts with your child should be an enjoyable and creative experience. If you are sitting down together trying to mass-produce crafts for the purpose of selling, you lose both the creativity involved and the enjoyment of doing something together. However, there are a couple of exceptions to this.

Doing crafts for fundraising purposes is one of those exceptions. Raising money for a cause or nonprofit organization can teach children great lessons. It is easier to get more people involved with making these crafts, which helps take away some of the monotony and stress of trying to do it all. It is also easier to sell crafts made to benefit a certain cause or nonprofit organization, because people

ELSEWHERE ON THE WEB

▶ I think I might have found the ultimate way to preserve your child's artwork while I was doing some research online. Check out what the people at Totally Out Of Hand can do with your child's drawings: www.totally outofhand.com. What they do is reproduce the artwork in solid sterling silver, completely by hand, by cutting out little pieces of silver, and then soldering them all together with a torch. These are not only wonderful gifts for mom, but also for grandma!

▶ **If you and your child would like to try crafting for charities, here are some worthwhile organizations to explore:** http://about.com/familycrafts/forcharity. **Most of these organizations accept completed projects and/or craft supplies. Some of these charities serve mainly their local areas, but you may be able to find or start something similar in your area. Also remember to check your local hospitals, shelters, etc. to see what they need.**

are more likely to spend their money if they know it's going to a good cause. I remember when my kids were little, they made simple beaded jewelry with their friends and then set up a card table and sold it on the street. We made it known that all of the money would be donated to our local food shelf, and they sold all of their inventory every day. You also may have more opportunities to sell your product if the proceeds are all being donated. Besides renting a booth at craft shows, you can investigate the possibilities of setting up a booth at church bazaars, school events, and even local stores.

The other exception is if you and your child have a craft you love to do together over and over again. Of course, there is no guarantee that they will be well received by the buying public, but trying to sell something you love to make is better than trying to make something that may sell better. If you enjoy making the product, selling it, or it not selling, will not be a big issue.

You can try to modify whatever it is you enjoy making in hopes that it sells better. Here are a few things to keep in mind or try:

- Would you buy it if someone else made it?
- Is it seasonal? Christmas ornaments and decorations would sell great in November or December, not in April or May. Try to make your product fit the season.
- Is it useful? There have been many times I have seen crafts at bazaars or craft shows and, while I loved the way they looked, I didn't buy them because there was no real purpose for them.
- Can they be personalized? Sometimes items that can be personalized with a name or date, such as hand-painted ornaments, are good sellers.

- Can you sell them for a low price? Anyone would be more willing to spend $3 on an item that they might use than $25.
- Are they a popular item at the moment? Trends change, and what might sell well one year may not sell at all the next. Page through craft magazines and visit other craft shows to see what sells well and then try to put your own unique spin on it.

Another option, rather than selling your completed craft projects, is to donate them. There are many organizations that accept donations of everything from homemade hats and scarves to teddy bears and blankets. Making a project for one or more of these organizations should be a meaningful experience for the entire family.

When my children were young and I ran my own day care business out of my home, we would make seasonal items to donate locally. These items ranged from Christmas-tree ornaments for local hospitals to Valentine's Day cards for residents of a nursing home. Not only did the kids get the joy of making the crafts, but they also got the joy of hand delivering them to grateful recipients!

Most important is to have fun. Don't force yourself or your child to sit down and make crafts. You want it to always be an enjoyable experience. If it gets to the point where trying to make crafts to sell, donate, or for any other reason is not enjoyable for you and your family, why do it?

WHAT'S HOT

▶ One thing you could try to make and sell at craft bazaars and even online are craft kits. You can gather together general supplies or make kits for specific crafts. This is an especially fun idea during the holiday season. You can make kits to make Christmas-tree ornaments or other seasonal items. Not only will you be making a little money, you will be encouraging other families to craft together! Here is some information about a craft kit I made: http://about.com/familycrafts/makecraftkit.

Get Linked

Cleaning up and staying organized are important parts of any crafting session. Plus, after your crafting session you have to figure out what to do with your finished crafts and also plan for your next craft session.

CRAFT-SUPPLY STORAGE IDEAS

If you are anything like me, you tend to have more crafting supplies than you have space. To help with storing and organizing your supplies, I thought I would share some of my favorite storage solutions and also some other unique storage ideas I ran across.

http://about.com/familycrafts/storageideas

MAKE A STORY SACK

Try this fun way to help kids to enjoy reading! Make a sack that contains a story book along with related craft ideas, games, and other fun stuff.

http://about.com/familycrafts/storysack

Appendix A

Glossary

acid free

Refers to paper and other items that do not contain acids. Acids can cause paper to discolor, become inflexible, and eventually turn brittle over time. Acid can also destroy photographs or various other elements if it comes in contact with them. If preserving your projects for years to come is important to you, you should avoid the use of paper and other items that are not labeled acid free.

aperture

A small, circular opening inside the lens of a camera that can change in diameter to control the amount of light reaching the camera's sensor as a picture is taken. The aperture diameter is expressed in f/stops; the lower the number, the larger the aperture. For instance, the aperture opening when set to f/2.8 is larger than at f/8. The aperture and shutter speed together control the total amount of light reaching the sensor.

archival

Refers to the ability of paper or other items to withstand the effects of time. In the case of printed items and photographs, it refers to the ability of the images to retain their color or blackness over long periods of time. In the case of paper, it is made with the intent of having an extended lifespan without discoloration or deterioration. Anything labeled archival should be acid free.

brayer

A brayer is a small hand roller, typically used to spread ink. They can be made of rubber, sponge, or acrylic. They can be used to spread ink onto stamps or directly onto surfaces. They can also be used with decoupage-type techniques to help remove wrinkles and excess glue.

ceramics

Refers to items made of clay that are shaped while moist and hardened by heat, also called firing, in a kiln.

cognitive skills

These are any mental skills that are used in the process of acquiring knowledge; these skills include reasoning, perception, and intuition.

diameter

This is the distance across a circle through its center.

easel

An easel is an upright support, usually a tripod, most often used to hold up an artist's canvas or paper while the painter is working, or to hold a completed painting for exhibition.

embellish

To decorate or add details to make projects more attractive by adding stitching, color, and any other objects.

embellishments

Refers to any item used for decorating purposes.

embossing

A technique which creates a raised (3D) image on paper. The two most popular ways to emboss are with the use of heat and powder or a stencil and stylus. You can also emboss on fabric.

ephemera

Technically, ephemera refers to printed matter that is usually read or used and discarded, such as ticket stubs, postcards, posters, greeting cards, etc., although it is also used to refer to other found objects used in crafts such as charms, keys, buttons, game pieces, beads, and ribbon.

essential oil

A highly concentrated oil having the odor or flavor of the plant from which it comes, mainly used in perfume, candles, soap, and flavorings.

f/stop #

A term used to indicate the speed of a lens. The smaller the f/number the greater amount of light passes through the lens.

fine-motor skills

The use of the small muscles of the body; includes the ability to manipulate small objects, transfer objects from hand to hand, and various hand-eye coordination tasks.

fluted

A border that resembles a scalloped edge.

found objects

Found objects are materials you find (such as pebbles, candy wrappers, or leaves), not buy (such as inks, paints, and crayons), to use in arts and crafts projects.

gauge

A unit of measurement used to describe the thickness of a wire. The lower the number, the thicker the wire. For instance, 22-gauge wire is much thinner than 12-gauge wire.

glossy

Having a smooth, gleaming, or shiny surface.

glycerin

Glycerin is a natural emollient and humectant that is a by-product of soap manufacturing. It is a clear, colorless, syrupy liquid. As a humectant and emollient, it absorbs moisture from the air, which helps keep moisture in whatever it is put into. It is often used in skin and hair-care products and soap making.

grout

A cement-type, sometimes colored, material used in the mosaic process to fill in the gaps between the individual tiles or pieces that make up the design.

laminate

A transparent plastic coating applied to paper or other objects to provide protection and give it a glossy finish. It sometimes comes in the form of a thin sheet of paper, as well as liquid form.

lignin free

Lignin-free paper is desirable when making scrapbooks and other projects where you want the paper to last for a long time. Paper that contains large amounts of lignin, such as newsprint, is very acidic and will turn yellow when exposed to light and humidity. Lignin is the natural bonding element which holds wood fibers together and can be removed in the pulping process.

matte

A dull, nonglossy finish. Often used when referring to a photograph, paper, or paint.

parallel

Refers to two or more lines that are separated at all points by the same distance.

pastels

Chalk-like sticks of powdered pigment held together with a gum-binding agent.

perpendicular

Two lines are perpendicular if the angle between them is 90 degrees (a right angle).

polyurethane

Used as a top coat on projects to form a tough, resistant coating.

pressing cloth

A piece of fabric used to protect garments and other items from steam and/or heat when pressing with an iron. It is placed between the iron and the garment being pressed.

soda ash

Also known as sodium carbonate, washing soda, or sal soda. It's a mild alkalai that enables the reaction between some dyes and fabric fibers. It makes for brighter, longer-lasting colors.

squeegee

A T-shaped cleaning tool with a rubber edge across the top. It is drawn across a surface to remove excess liquid.

terra cotta

A term used to describe ceramic products made from a hard, waterproof clay fired at low temperatures. Terra cotta pieces are usually a brownish-orange color, and unglazed.

tesserae

The small pieces of stone, glass, or other objects that are pieced together to create a mosaic.

translucent

Partially transparent, allowing some light to pass through.

transparency

When something is transparent it means you can see through it. A transparency is also a clear, plastic sheet.

tulle

This is a fine, mesh fabric used commonly for bridal veils, etc. Tulle is usually made of nylon, silk, or rayon.

Appendix B

Other Sites

Activity Idea Place

This site hosts over 2,400 activity ideas for Early Childhood Education professionals and parents. www.123child.com

Craft Bits

This site has a wonderful selection of craft projects and informational articles. One of my favorite online sites. www.craftbits.com

Danielle's Place

A large selection of craft projects, many of which are Bible-based and are great to use in Sunday School, Vacation Bible School, preschool, and home school. www.daniellesplace.com

DLTK's Printable Crafts for Kids

This site features many unique crafts, and most of the projects include printable templates. It also has many printable coloring pages. www.dltk-kids.com

Holiday Crafter

This site offers several great crafts you can make to celebrate many of the more well-known holidays. www.holidaycrafter.com

I-Craft

This Web site is hosted by the Craft and Hobby Association and has a selection of free projects and information. This site is made for crafters, teachers, and parents. www.i-craft.com

Imagination Factory

This is an award-winning arts and crafts site for teachers, kids, and parents, that teaches ways to creatively recycle to make crafts. www.kid-at-art.com

Making Friends

This site has a large selection of craft ideas for kids. The drop-down menus help you get to exactly what you are looking for. This is a commercial site, and I think it's fun that you can buy the supplies for each project while browsing. www.makingfriends.com

Appendix C

Further Reading

Creative Computer Crafts by Marcelle Costanza

Not only does this book offer dozens of unique craft projects, it teaches you more about your computer and how to use it to make crafts.

Funky Junk by Renee Schwarz

This book shows you how to turn nuts, bolts, washers, and other hardware into funky crafts.

Jumbo Book of Art by Irene Luxbacher

This book is great for anyone who ever feels the urge to create! Learn techniques and the tools you will need to make creative masterpieces.

Jumbo Book of Crafts by Judy Ann Sadler

This book has more than 150 craft ideas to choose from. It is broken into five sections: Things for Your Room, Things to Wear, Gifts to Make, Special Days, and Old-Time Crafts.

Make Spectacular Books by Sue Astroth

Whether you are an experienced scrapbooker, paper crafter, or quilter or a beginner, you're sure to be able to find the perfect project in this book about making books using fabric and a few other supplies.

Photo Fun: Print Your Own Fabrics for Quilts and Crafts by Cyndy Lyle Rymer

This book has so many inspiring projects I couldn't wait to try them out! As popular as digital cameras are these days, the projects and ideas in this book offer great ways to use digital photos.

Index

Tooth saver, 83
Tote bags, 116–18
Tracing paper, 7
Trash, crafts using, 69–84
Treasure chest, 230
Tree of thanks, 180
Turkey candy or nut holder, 179
Tween crafts, 62–66
Tweezers, 6

U

Umbrella picture, 187–88
Utility knife, 5

V

Valentine's Day butterfly, 185
Vase, 246–47
Vellum, 7
Volcano, 124–25

W

Watercolors, 8
Watermelon picture, 194
Wax paper, 6
Wearable crafts, 103–19
Wiggle eyes, 6
Wind sock, 125–26
Winter crafts, 180–85
Wire, 10, 74
Wire cutters, 11
Writing instruments, 2–3, 7–8

X

Xyron, 13

Y

Yard games, 153–54
Yard projects, 96–99
Yarn, 6

Z

Zip-top bags, 256